ON THE EMPLOYMENT
OF CHILDREN IN FACTORIES

The Development of Industrial Society Series

Leonard Horner

ON THE EMPLOYMENT
OF CHILDREN
IN FACTORIES

and Other Works
in the United Kingdom and in
Some Foreign Countries

IRISH UNIVERSITY PRESS
Shannon   Ireland

First edition London 1840

This I U P reprint is a photolithographic facsimile of the first edition and is unabridged, retaining the original printer's imprint.

© *1971 Irish University Press Shannon Ireland*

All forms of micropublishing
© *Irish University Microforms Shannon Ireland*

ISBN 0 7165 1596 2

T M MacGlinchey Publisher
Irish University Press Shannon Ireland

PRINTED IN THE REPUBLIC OF IRELAND BY
ROBERT HOGG PRINTER TO IRISH UNIVERSITY PRESS

The Development of Industrial Society Series

This series comprises reprints of contemporary documents and commentaries on the social, political and economic upheavals in nineteenth-century England.

England, as the first industrial nation, was also the first country to experience the tremendous social and cultural impact consequent on the alienation of people in industrialized countries from their rural ancestry. The Industrial Revolution which had begun to intensify in the mid-eighteenth century, spread swiftly from England to Europe and America. Its effects have been far-reaching: the growth of cities with their urgent social and physical problems; greater social mobility; mass education; increasingly complex administration requirements in both local and central government; the growth of democracy and the development of new theories in economics; agricultural reform and the transformation of a way of life.

While it would be pretentious to claim for a series such as this an in-depth coverage of all these aspects of the new society, the works selected range in content from *The Hungry Forties* (1904), a collection of letters by ordinary working people describing their living conditions and the effects of mechanization on their day-to-day lives, to such analytical studies as Leone Levi's *History of British Commerce* (1880) and *Wages and Earnings of the Working Classes* (1885); M. T. Sadler's *The Law of Population* (1830); John Wade's radical documentation of government corruption, *The Extraordinary Black Book* (1831); C. Edward Lester's trenchant social investigation, *The Glory and Shame of England* (1866); and many other influential books and pamphlets.

The editor's intention has been to make available important contemporary accounts, studies and records, written or compiled by men and women of integrity and scholarship whose reactions to the growth of a new kind of society are valid touchstones for today's reader. Each title (and the particular edition used) has been chosen on a twofold basis (1) its intrinsic worth as a record or commentary, and (2) its contribution to the development of an industrial society. It is hoped that this collection will help to increase our understanding of a people and an epoch.

The Editor
Irish University Press

ON THE

EMPLOYMENT OF CHILDREN,

IN

FACTORIES AND OTHER WORKS.

LONDON:
Printed by A. SPOTTISWOODE,
New-Street-Square.

ON THE

EMPLOYMENT OF CHILDREN,

IN

FACTORIES AND OTHER WORKS

IN

THE UNITED KINGDOM,

AND IN SOME

FOREIGN COUNTRIES.

BY

LEONARD HORNER, F.R.S.

INSPECTOR OF FACTORIES.

LONDON:
LONGMAN, ORME, BROWN, GREEN, AND LONGMANS,
BANCKS & CO., MANCHESTER; BAINES & NEWSOME, LEEDS;
AND DAVID ROBERTSON, GLASGOW.
1840.

PREFACE.

It is hoped that Parliament, during the present Session, will be again called upon to legislate in behalf of the children employed in factories; and, for the sake of the many who are unprotected in consequence of the defects in the existing law, as well as for the sake of the honest mill-owner who strictly obeys the law, but is exposed to unfair competition from the too easy evasions of it by his less scrupulous neighbour, it will be a matter of great regret if another Session should be allowed to terminate without an amending Act having passed.

The chief purpose of the present publication is to show, and especially to our manufacturers, that it is not now in this country alone that the employment of children in factories is restricted by law. The inhumanity, injustice, and impolicy of extorting labour from children unsuitable to their age and strength,— of subjecting them, in truth, to the hardships of slavery (for they are not free agents), — have been condemned by the public voice in other countries; and their governments have either already applied, or are now engaged in preparing, a remedy for this vice of modern times. I have entered into a somewhat lengthened detail of the recent proceedings in France; for they bring forcibly before us the baneful consequences of this system, and give as it

were a reflection of that which did exist, and in
some branches of manufacture, and in mines, does
still exist, in our own country.   I have also felt that
the wise and humane sentiments expressed in the
several Reports, and in the speeches delivered in
the Chamber of Peers when the question was discussed, may stimulate our legislators not to relax
until the evil in every shape be put down, and may
reconcile our manufacturers to the interference to
which they are subjected, when they see that the
example of England has been followed by other
nations, and that the overruling necessity of restricting the labour of children has been admitted, after
the most calm and dispassionate inquiries.

In the introductory observations I have alluded
to some of the causes why the law of 1833 was
passed in so imperfect a state, with so many facilities
for evading its most important enactments, as a
warning to guard against similar risks of imperfection
in the amending Act.   I have pointed out the necessity of restricting the labour of the children
within more definite limits than are fixed by the
present Act; and I have urged the justice and policy
of extending these restrictions to other kinds of employment besides that in Factories; for, until that is
done, the law will be felt to be partial and unfair, and
will only imperfectly attain its object.

London, June 3. 1840.

CONTENTS.

EMPLOYMENT

OF

CHILDREN IN FACTORIES,

&c.

I. *Introductory Observations.*

THE law which was passed in 1833, to regulate the labour of children and young persons in the mills and factories of the United Kingdom, and is now in force, has been productive of much good; it has put an end to a large proportion of the evils which made the interference of the legislature then necessary. But it has not done nearly all the good that was intended; it has not by any means accomplished all the purposes for which it was passed. The failures have mainly arisen from defects in the law itself; not in the principles it lays down, but in the machinery which was constructed for the purpose of carrying the principles into operation. The Act was passed at a late period of the session, amidst a great deal of excitement on the subject, and when there was no opportunity of considering the details of the measure with due calmness and deliberation. There was this further source of error, that it was in some degree legislating in the dark; a great part of the mechanism adopted was entirely of a novel description, of a kind that had

never been tried in former factory acts; and after
it was set to work, much of it was found to
have been ill contrived, and some positively so
bad that it obstructed, and to a great degree prevented, the attainment of the object. Many, and
some of the worst, of the defects cannot be laid to
the charge of the original framers of the Bill, but
were caused by the interference of members who
were not aware what they were doing, and who were,
in most instances, prompted by others. It was very
natural, and it was to be expected, that the mill-
owners should be stirring at such a moment, and that
they should endeavour to make the law press as
lightly as possible upon themselves. But too much
weight was attached to their broad assertions,
(much more than the parties themselves would
now claim for them), that if such and such things
were done, the most serious consequences would
ensue to the manufacturing interest, the great
strength of the country. They spoke with the confident tone of superior knowledge and experience;
used technical terms, unintelligible, and, therefore,
having a somewhat mystical import to those they
were addressing; and the legislators, with a very
natural timidity and caution, did not venture to disregard altogether remonstrances so strongly made.
" In the House of Commons legislation general
principles are held in absolute distrust : nothing is
deemed certain but what is individual and special.
Every motive has therefore equal weight; every
trifling inconvenience takes rank as an insuperable
objection; and the question is carried by some
side-wind — by some contingent inducement that
has nothing necessarily to do with the merits of the

case. This is the field in which every indirect
manœuvre can be practised, if not without detection,
without inconvenient exposure."*

Had all the remonstrances which were made been
attended to, the children would have been left with
but a scanty measure of protection; and we may in
some degree judge of the value of those which were
yielded to, by the experience of the working of those
enactments which were persisted in. It was confidently predicted that, by limiting the employment
of children of eleven years of age to eight hours
a day, the most serious losses would accrue; that
when, in the following year, the Act should apply to
children of twelve, the difficulties and evil consequences would be vastly increased; that if it were
attempted to enforce the restriction as far as thirteen,
a very large proportion of the mills in the country
must of necessity stop. Government were applied
to, to prevent the impending evil; the inspectors
were appealed to by the Government, and they stated
that the assertions had been so often and so confidently
made to them, that they could not venture to set up
their opinions and their then limited experience in
opposition to them. The President of the Board of
Trade, Mr. Thompson, was prevailed upon to propose to Parliament that the restriction to eight hours'
daily work should be limited to children under twelve
years of age; but happily Parliament was firm, and
would not yield. And what was the result? Not a
single mill throughout the United Kingdom stopped
a day for want of hands. I have not a doubt that
the assertions were, in many cases, made in perfect

* *Athenæum*, May 2. 1840; in the Review of Sir Samuel
Romilly's Memoirs.

honesty, and with a firm persuasion that the consequences predicted would ensue ; but it ought to be a lesson to Parliament, in the progress of the amending Act, to listen with "a very academic faith" to statements of dangers to trade, when they are considering how they shall make the protection to the children against excessive labour, and the provisions for their education, more effective than they have hitherto proved by the present law. It will be of great consequence to look with a jealous eye upon all proposed changes of phrases, and even of single words, by interested parties. They may seem harmless to those unacquainted with the practical working of the act ; but they may have this effect, as we know by experience, that an important enactment may thereby be rendered inoperative. For example : there is, I believe, no doubt that it was intended, that all mills should be closed on Good Friday and Christmas-day, the same as on a Sunday, in England and Ireland ; but in consequence of a single word, the clause has been rendered almost nugatory.

It is, however, very satisfactory to know, that the act is now viewed by a great majority of the respectable mill-owners, their managers, and, as far as I have had an opportunity of learning, by the most considerate and best disposed among the work-people themselves, with a very different feeling from what it was at first. I have had abundant testimony that the law is not only not felt to be oppressive and detrimental to trade, but, on the contrary, has been productive of great good, by introducing a steadiness and a regularity which did not exist before. Many mill-owners have said to me, — "We find no fault with the Act, except that we are not all placed by it on the same footing, in consequence of the evasions which our neighbours may and do practise with impunity; and if the law will not reach them, it ought to be made to do so." It may fairly be said, that the experience of the last six years has incontestably proved, that the limitation of nine years, below which children are not allowed to work in cotton, woollen, and flax mills; the restriction in the same mills upon all between nine and thirteen from working more than eight hours a day, and upon those between thirteen and eighteen from working more than twelve hours a day; the prohibition of night-work as regards children, and its limitation in the case of young persons; and the enforcement of the daily attendance of the children at school, are perfectly compatible with a successful carrying on of the manufacture; and that the records required to be kept, and the regulations for securing and ascertaining the due observance of the law, do not occasion any vexatious or unreasonable trouble, nor involve any risks which the most moderate attention may not completely guard against. That it has in some degree increased the price of infant labour is true, but no one was so irrational as to suppose that it would not. Children were overworked because a profit was made from their extra labour: that unrighteous source of profit has been cut off, as it ought to be; but that the cost of production has been increased by these restrictions upon children, beyond a very trifling amount, few will venture to maintain.

The defects of the existing law have been repeatedly pointed out by the inspectors in their reports; and the Bill that was brought in by Government last year, but withdrawn on account of the then advanced period of the session, remedied nearly the whole of these defects; although, in my opinion, not all of them, nor in the best way. The evidence given before the Committee, now sitting, has made the imperfections still more apparent; and there is, therefore, every reason to expect, that a much better Act will be obtained than would have passed before this late inquiry took place. Judging from the Government Bill of last year, it is not very probable that any material extension of the principles of the present Act will be made, except in the case of silk mills. It was agreed in the committee on the Bill, last year, to bring them under the full operation of the Act, which they are not at present: children are admitted into silk mills at as early an age as the owner chooses to employ them, and sometimes they are employed as young as six; they are also allowed to work ten hours a day, and are not required to attend school. There never was any sound reason for these exemptions *in favour of silk mill-owners*, and there is none now. If the question were, "What does the interest of the silk mill-owners require?" and if the labour of the children were to be accommodated accordingly, we know very well what the answer of the masters would be; but the question to be asked is: "What does the interest *of the children* require?" And Parliament must tell the masters, that they must accommodate themselves the best way they can to the conditions upon which alone the State will allow them to purchase infant labour; and those conditions must be such as will effectually protect the health of the children, and secure some education for them; but, at the same time, with as little incovenience as possible to them, as to all other mill-owners, and to the workers of all ages employed in the factories.

It will be seen, on reading the reports of the Inspectors and the evidence given before the Committee, that the restriction of the labour of children between nine and thirteen years of age to eight hours a day is frequently evaded with impunity. The causes of these evasions are, *first*, that there is a range of fifteen hours within the extreme limits of which these eight hours may be taken; and, *secondly*, that the child may be worked at any time of the day, at any intervals within that range. Where they work with relays of three children, each working eight hours, instead of two above thirteen, working twelve hours each, and where the system is regularly attended to, it does quite well; but in the majority of instances, at present, where they employ children under thirteen years of age, they have no relays; *they say* that they manage to do without them the remaining four hours. They are frequently sent out at the most uncertain and irregular times, according as they can be spared; and as that varies often from day to day, so it may easily be seen to what evasions such a system must give rise; accordingly, it is perpetually happening, that the adults, whom the children assist, keep them beyond the time when they ought to be sent out. This also happens even when they employ relays of three for two, as above described; for the times for the children leaving off frequently occurring while the adult is at work, and not when *he* stops for a meal, the children are kept, both designedly and undesignedly, beyond the legal limits. Various forms of registers have been tried to prevent this; but the best of them supply an imperfect check, where there is a disposition to evade the law.

There appears to be but one practicable way in which a limitation of the hours of the children's labour can be secured : it might not in all cases be effectual, but it would be so in a very great majority ; and it would be, at all events, a vast improvement on the present system. It is this, that no child under thirteen years of age shall be allowed to work more than half a day, the day to be divided by the general dinner hour of the factory. There would thus be a morning set and an afternoon set of children. The dinner is a marked break : it is the longest interval, and, in general, it is about the middle of the day. But in as much as the dinner hour varies, in different parts of the kingdom, that circumstance must not be lost sight of. In a great number of places in England it is from twelve to one o'clock; in others, from half past twelve to half past one ; in others, from one to two. Where they begin work at half past five in the morning, and dine at twelve, allowing half an hour for breakfast, there is an equal division of the working day of twelve hours : where they begin at the same hour, but dine at one o'clock, the morning set would work seven hours, and the afternoon set five hours. Therefore, besides the enactment that no child shall work more than one half of the day, and that the half day shall be either wholly before dinner or wholly after it, it will be necessary to declare that no child shall be allowed to work more than seven hours in any one day, or more than forty-two hours in the week. In Scotland, where work-people generally dine at two o'clock, it would be necessary that the hour in the factories should be altered, so as not to be later than one o'clock.* It seems irrational not to permit the children to work partly before and partly after dinner, and a member unacquainted with the subject, with the best possible motives, might rise in his place when the Bill is in Committee, and appear most reasonable in suggesting that permission for that purpose should be given: but were this allowed, it would at once open the door to endless frauds; it is therefore a concession that must be made, for the sake of securing an uniform obedience to this, the most important, part of the law.

The advantages to the children of thus limiting them to half a day's work would be very great. They would have less labour and less confinement. The morning set, when they begin at half past five, and dine at one o'clock, would never work more than seven hours a day, and forty-two hours in the week; while the afternoon set would not exceed five hours a day, and twenty-seven hours a week: and a considerate master would place as many as possible of the youngest children in the afternoon set. Those who worked in the morning would have done with the factory at noon: they might throw off their working dresses, be washed, dine, and go to school in the afternoon; and have plenty of time in the open air eight months of the year. The afternoon set would not be obliged to rise very early in the morning: they would go to

---

* I have understood that it was originally intended that children under thirteen years of age should be limited to six hours a day; but an ingenious mill-owner of Glasgow, recollecting the hours in his own factory, suggested the plan of working by relays of three for two; and showed that by a very simple casting of the hours, *every* child might work eight hours, instead of one child working eight hours, and another the remaining four.

school in the forenoon; have time for play; and, putting on their working dresses, would go to the factory at one or two o'clock.

The children, at present, are often worked at hours very unsuitable for their education, in order to meet the convenience of the older hands; so that the time allotted for their going to school is sometimes six in the morning, at others half past seven in the evening. It very frequently happens that they are sent before nine in the morning, and after five o'clock in the afternoon; and therefore they have to go to some inferior teacher, as the hours in regular schools are usually between nine and five. But if there were a morning and an afternoon set, two or even three hours of the best schools could be had between nine and twelve for the one, and between one and five for the other. There would, besides, be no difficulty in getting them admitted to those good schools from which the masters now exclude them, on account of their dirty working dresses.

If this plan were adopted, the limit of admission might safely be lowered to *eight* years instead of nine, as it is at present; for no child of eight years of age would get any harm by working half a day in the factory, especially in the afternoon; and it would make up to many parents for the diminution of the wages by the reduction from eight hours' work, by enabling them to have another child employed. There would be a reduction in the payments to individuals, but the mass of parents would lose nothing, for the manufacturer would pay the same amount of wages as before, only he would distribute it among a greater number of children.

To the masters, the advantages would be these:—

their adult spinners would never be working without their full complement of young hands; the keeping of the record of the children's time of working would be greatly simplified, and the risk of infractions of the law by their work-people would be greatly diminished.

All with whom I have spoken on this subject agree in thinking that it is the most generally practicable plan: a considerable number of mill-owners are already acting upon it, and several have done so for a long time. Every one who has tried it finds the advantages of it, over every other mode of employing children. My belief is, that, with few exceptions, it would give satisfaction to mill-owners at once, and that it would not be long before parents would generally admit the beneficial change it had produced.

It is not my purpose, in this publication, to point out, in detail, the defects of the existing Factory Act, or to give my opinion as to the remedies which ought to be applied. The Committee gave me an opportunity of stating both, and therefore I should only repeat what is already contained in my printed evidence. Besides, the Bill that was brought forward last year shows that the government are anxious to correct all the defects in the law; and, as far as possible, to meet the wishes of those who are most earnest in pleading the cause of the poor children; by affording them full protection as regards their health, and by making such provision for their education as the circumstances of the country, and the state of public opinion on this question, will admit of; while, at the same time, they wish to avoid laying any greater restraints upon the mill-owner than the exigency of the case calls for, in order to secure an uniform obedience to the law, and so protect the honest manufacturer against an unfair competition, in the same market, by a less scrupulous neighbour.

My chief object on the present occasion is to show, both to our legislators and to our manufacturers, that it is not now in this country alone that the labour of children is restricted. The example of England, and particularly in passing the more efficient Act of 1833, has not been lost upon the philanthropists of other countries in Europe. It is most honourable to those countries, and it must be cheering to the friends of humanity to see it, that, at a time when many of their manufactures, and particularly those in which they enter into competition with us, may be said to be in a comparatively youthful, if not an infant state, they have not hesitated to come forward to stop that oppression of the children, which, by the rapid growth of their manufactures, was becoming daily more widely spread. It is, moreover, most creditable to France, that some of the manufacturers themselves were the first to urge the necessity of this legislative interference. The measures which other governments have taken, or are now taking, cannot fail to have the effect of strengthening Parliament in their determination to make our own legislation in behalf of unprotected children more and more effective ; and of reconciling our manufacturers to the restrictions, when they see that other countries, which they look upon with some alarm as formidable rivals, are subject to laws quite as stringent as that by which their own manufactures are regulated. I trust that by thus making the proceedings in other countries more extensively known in our own than they probably would otherwise have been, I shall forward this most just and humane, and, therefore, most wise and politic object.

Prussia, as will be seen by the law which she passed more than a year ago, has extended protection, not only to the children in factories, but to those employed in some other branches of industry. The same is the case, and to a still greater extent, in the Bill which has passed the Chamber of Peers in France, and is now under the consideration of the Chamber of Deputies. A copy of this Bill will be found in the sequel. This proceeding in the French Chambers comes most opportunely, at this moment, in support of the views entertained by our own government, that silk mills ought to be subject to all the provisions of the Factory Act. France, which is acknowledged on all hands to be our great rival in the silk trade, makes no exception in favour of that or of any other description of manufacture, and therefore that argument, which has been so strongly urged as a reason why children from six to thirteen years of age *must* be allowed to work ten hours every day, and *cannot* be allowed any time either for education or healthful exercise, happily falls to the ground.

If we have had the proud distinction of having been acknowledged by other great powers in Europe to have been the first to lead the way in this humane and wise course, it is to be hoped that we shall not be backward in following the example which they have set before us, by extending the protecting arm of the law to neglected, oppressed, and helpless children, much more widely than has yet been done. To be just to those branches of industry which are now subject to restriction, it is indispensable that, in all employments which can be brought within the reach of a law, the labour of children, *who are let out for hire*, should be restricted. At present a cotton spinner who cannot employ children under nine years of age, or those between nine and thirteen more than eight hours a day, finds his next neighbour, a calico printer, working them at any age and for any length of time; by day or by night, without restraint of any kind; and he justly complains that he is subjected to partial legislation.* It would not be difficult to draw up a tolerably long list of employments, in which children are made to work a most unreasonable length of time ; and in many of the works the processes are exceedingly prejudicial to health. In the evidence recently given before the Committee on Factories, it is shown that, in the lace mills of Nottingham, children from nine to fifteen years of age are frequently employed twenty hours, from four in the morning to twelve at night. (*Second Report*, pp. 57. and 72.) It has been again and again said to me, " Why does not the law interfere in the case of the children employed in the print works, where they are much worse off than in the cotton mills, working from an early hour in the morning to late at night, and often all night ? Why does it not prevent the atrocities in coal pits ? " † I myself spoke to a boy of eleven years of age who had worked in a coal-pit in Lanca-

* The abuses that are said to prevail in calico print works, with respect to the employment of children, calls loudly for parliamentary inquiry. It appears, from some inquiries I have myself made, to be a common practice to make children of *six* and *seven* years of age work twelve hours continuously, sometimes more, and even in the middle of the night, in the depth of winter, for weeks together. For farther particulars, see Appendix A.

† See Appendix B.

shire, who told me that he went down at six in the morning, and did not come up again till four in the afternoon; that his occupation below ground was to drag a basket of coals to which he was yoked, in a place where he could not stand upright, and walking in water above his ankles. It has been stated to me that, in some parts of England they make little children creep into places not above eighteen inches high, to get out the coal, where the seams are so thin, that to cut away the stone with which the coal is interstratified, so as to make room for a grown man to work, the coal would not pay.

I have heard it said that to interfere to the extent here proposed would be humanity running riot, and exceeding all reasonable bounds; that it would be an encroachment on parental rights, and would be at variance with all sound principles of legislation. So far from thinking this to be the case, it appears to me that the interposition of the legislature in behalf of children is justified by the most cold and severe principles of political economy; and the alleged interference with parental authority by such legislation is a mere sophism.

The wealth of a country surely depends, in no inconsiderable degree, on the people who are engaged in works of industry, being capable of performing the greatest possible amount of labour in a given time, without impairing their health; for it will cost a great deal less to maintain, in food, clothes, and lodging, two strong healthy men employed to perform a piece of work, than would be required if we had to employ three men to do the same work, because of their inferior muscular powers. To cultivate the intelligence, and increase the probability of useful inventions, by improving the natural faculties of the working classes, must also be considered a source of national wealth; and to be spared the expense of the repression and punishment of crime seems no less clearly an important element in national prosperity. Now unless every possible chance be given *to the child* of growing up healthy and strong, unless his natural intelligence be cultivated and drawn out, unless moral and religious principles be early implanted in him, so as to become a part of his nature, what chance have we of his growing up to be a healthy, strong, intelligent, ingenious, honest, and right-principled man, a useful and orderly citizen? No one doubts that a large proportion of those deluded people who followed the Chartist leaders were betrayed into acts of violence and lawless outrage, more from their deplorable ignorance than from any other cause; that many of them had been utterly neglected in their youth; and that they had probably worked, when they were children, from twelve to fourteen hours a day, in factories, and other branches of manufacture.

It is in vain that we establish schools, if the children have no time to attend them: if the children of our working classes are to be raised from their present degraded condition, by means of education, it is obvious that it can only be done by securing to them, in the first instance, the time necessary for it. If, in order to be allowed to make a profit by the labour of children, it were made a condition, that the child shall not thereby be deprived of the means of obtaining a suitable education, it would be so far an adoption of a compulsory system; but one both gentle and reasonable, and, at the same time, most extensively efficacious.

I have heard it proposed, even by sensible men, but who evidently had not given much consideration to the subject when they advanced such an opinion, that if children at nine or ten years of age are able to read and write, they ought to be allowed to work, without being obliged to attend school any longer. This is taking a very narrow view of education indeed; it reminds me that, within the last year, I heard a worthy lady, the wife of a dignitary of the church, say, that in her opinion all the learning which the working classes require is to know the Creed, the Lord's Prayer, and the Ten Commandments; and I believe that she by no means stands single in that opinion. I am very far from undervaluing Infants' Schools, but I would not accept them in lieu of all others, for any class of the people: the instruction given in them, and the habits of attention and order which the children acquire, are an excellent preparation for the education that is to come after. It cannot be too often repeated, so long as the delusion is so prevalent as it is at present, that a child who knows how to read is not educated, but has only made the first step in that intellectual, moral, and religious training, which alone constitutes education, and which can only be given by a long-continued attendance in a good school.

It has been also proposed that children should not be allowed to work at all until they can read, and that a farther advance should be made in education before a child of thirteen should be allowed to work more than eight hours a day. If good schools were to be found every where, and had been some time in operation, it might, and perhaps would, be expedient to impose these conditions; but it could not be done at present, in this country, without great injustice in many cases.

As to the alleged encroachment on parental authority — if the parent does his duty to his child, if he takes due care of his health, and gives him such advantages of education as are within his reach, he will not know of the existence of the law, for he will have already done all that the law requires. Parental authority confers no right on a father wantonly to mutilate the little finger of his child; ought he to be permitted to do what is a thousand times worse, to enfeeble him and spread disease through his whole frame, to leave him as low in intelligence as a brute, and to infect him with the most dangerous of all pestilences, a corrupt, depraved mind? If the father has his natural rights, so has the child; and if the father robs him of these, the State must become his guardian, and restore them to him.

The increasing tendency to employ children, and for such a number of hours daily as is ruinous both to their physical and moral condition, in order to cheapen production, in almost all branches of industry, and the growing, unnatural, and vicious practice of parents making their children work, to enable themselves to live in idleness and profligacy, can only be checked by some law of general application. I cannot see that it would be in any respect inconsistent with sound principle, to pass a general law to the following effect; applicable to all children who are let out to work for hire, away from the houses of their parents:

1. That no child under eight years of age shall be allowed to work in any description of labour whatsoever.

2. That no child under thirteen years of age shall be allowed to work more than *half a day;* the day being divided by the ordinary dining hour of the working classes, in the place where the child works.

3. That no child under thirteen years of age shall be allowed to work before five o'clock in the morning, or after eight o'clock at night.

4. That the parent, or other person deriving benefit from the wages of the child, shall be obliged to lay aside a certain portion of the child's own earnings for its own education; and shall be required to produce weekly to the employer a certificate, in proof that the child has attended school for at least two hours daily, on five days of the preceding week, until he has completed his thirteenth year.

To secure obedience to such a law, some form of inspection would be necessary; what that ought to be would be a matter of subsequent consideration, as it would have to be different, according to the description of employment, and the localities. But until such inspecting systems were contrived, although much evasion might be practised, the existence of the general law, accompanied with adequate penalties in cases of contravention, and with the power of these being prosecuted with little trouble and expense, could not fail to operate as a terror on many, and would put a stop to an immense amount of suffering among the children of the humbler and poorer classes.

II. Proceedings in France, *preliminary to the Introduction of the Law to regulate the Labour of Children in Factories and other Works.*

Being in Paris in the autumn of 1838, I learned from my friend M. Francois Delessert*, that he and others had been watching very attentively the operation of our Factory Act, and had come to the determination to endeavour to obtain legislative protection for the same class of children in France. He put into my hands some documents which abundantly proved that interference in their behalf was as necessary as it had ever been in England. About the same time I received from Dr. Villermé a copy of his Report to the Academy of Moral and Political Sciences, containing an account of an inquiry in 1835 and 1836, instituted by direction of the Academy, and intrusted to Dr. Villermé, and M. Benoiston de Chateauneuf, into the moral and physical condition of the operatives employed in the silk, cotton, and woollen factories of France.

This work contains many sad pictures of the demoralised condition of the work-people in many of the manufacturing districts, and of the oppression to which the children are often subjected. The following are some of the statements of Dr. Villermé, and

* Banker, and member of the Chamber of Deputies. He and his brother, Baron Benjamin Delessert, have long been known for their active and enlightened exertions in the cause of humanity.

many of a like nature might be extracted from his
pages : —

" From what has been said, it will be seen, that many
master manufacturers, I might say the greater number, give
themselves no concern either as to the feelings, the morals, or
the fate of their work-people, looking upon them only as mere
productive machines. Yet I have often heard these same
masters complain of their workmen, especially of their steal-
ing the raw material, and of their spirit of hatred and ingratitude, and of the debased and corrupt principles by which they
are guided. But has he a right to complain of meeting with
ingratitude and hatred who never makes any inquiries either
about them or their families in times of sickness ? who never
utters a kind encouraging word to them, who never sees them
but in his own workshop, never addresses them, except, per-
chance, in some insolent monosyllable ?" (P. 38.)

After speaking of the hours of work extending to
thirteen and fourteen daily, and of the working in the
night, he says, —

" These working days seem to me to be certainly very long,
I might almost say excessive ; and the more so that all work
alike, whatever the age may be. They are one of the principal causes, if not the principal cause, of the sufferings of
the children, and even of some of the adults of the poorest
class. Sad as their condition is, that of the children in a
vast number of our manufactories is such as ought to excite
our pity ; for being frequently the victims of the profligacy
and improvidence of their parents, they ought not to partake
of the wretched consequences of their misconduct. In Alsace,
many of these unhappy creatures belong to Swiss and German
families who have been ruined, whom the hope of bettering
their condition leads there ; and thus they bring their labour
in competition with that of the inhabitants of the country.
Their first care, after having obtained employment, is to find
a lodging-place ; but the rents in the manufacturing towns
and villages immediately adjoining are so high, that they are

often obliged to live at the distance of a league, and even a league and a half. The poor children, many of whom are scarcely seven years old, and some even younger, have to take from their sleep and their meal hours whatever time is required to traverse that long and weary road, in the morning to get to the factory, in the evening to get home. This state of misery is particularly observable at Mulhausen, a town which, in spite of its rapid increase, does not afford dwellings for those whom its manufactures are daily drawing to it. It is therefore a sad sight to witness the work-people coming in, in the morning, from all the country round; and, above all, to see that multitude of emaciated, ghastly children, covered with rags, walking barefoot through the mud, carrying in their hand, or, if it rains, under their clothes, which are rendered impermeable to wet by the grease that has fallen from the machinery upon them, the piece of black bread, which is to be all the food they are to have until they get home again. The children employed in all the cotton spinning and weaving establishments of the Upper Rhine, and in the factories of the same description in other parts of France, are not, in general, it is true, in so miserable a condition; but every where pale and feeble, languid in their motions, and quiet in their sports, they present a picture of misery, suffering, and depression, which form a striking contrast with the ruddy complexion, the chubby faces, the saucy looks, and all those signs of joyous health which are observable in children of the same age, when we pass from a manufacturing into an agricultural district." (P. 62.)

"To judge how excessive is this labour of the children in the factories, one has only to recollect that it is unlawful to employ galley slaves more than twelve hours a day, and these twelve must be broken by two hours for meals, reducing the actual labour to ten hours a day; while the young people of whom I speak have to toil thirteen hours, and sometimes thirteen hours and a half, independent of their meal times. It may be said that the labour of a stone mason, of a carpenter, of a labourer, is more fatiguing; but these are men, in the vigour of life, earning wages sufficient to give them plenty of good food; whereas those whose sufferings I am now detailing are poor children of from six to thirteen years of age, a prey to every want, and many of them employed in unhealthy processes." (P. 64.)

" It is not the efforts of individual mill-owners that will remedy such abuses; the most benevolent mill-owner may have a neighbour exactly the reverse. It would require a holy alliance of all the manufacturers, not only of the country where they live, but in the country where their commodities are sold, to put down the enormities I have described, instead of making them a source of profit. But most assuredly such disinterestedness is not to be looked for : no class of society has hitherto offered such an instance, either in France or elsewhere. The only remedy for this destruction of children, of these homicidal proceedings, is to be found in a law which shall fix a *maximum* of daily labour, according to the age of the labourer." (P. 67.)

From that time I have had several communications with M. Delessert on the operation of our own law, and on what was going on in France, leading to legislative measures ; but more particularly within the last three months, since the government presented to the Chamber of Peers a bill (*projet de loi*) to regulate the labour of children in manufactories. He has sent me a variety of documents, both manuscript and printed, containing the history of the past and present state of the question; and from these materials I shall now proceed to give a brief account of the steps by which the French Chambers have been led to adopt active measures for the suppression of these evils, together with such extracts from the official documents, and from the speeches during the discussion in the Chamber of Peers, as appear to me to bear most strongly upon the general question of the justice and expediency of a law of this nature, and as most deserving the attention of the employers of children in our own country, and of those who are to amend our law for their protection.

As early as the year 1828 the Industrial Society of Mulhausen * called the attention of the government to the fearful abuses to which children were exposed by premature employment and excessive labour in the factories; but it was not till 1833 that the government responded to this benevolent appeal from that society, composed of men whose private interests would seem rather to have led them to stand forward in defence of unlimited freedom in settling the conditions under which they were to employ their work-people. The Minister of Public Instruction undertook to collect the information necessary for resolving this question of legislative interference; but his inquiries led to no result.

In 1835, the manufacturers of Mulhausen, through the medium of their Chamber of Commerce, again solicited the government to turn their attention to the subject. In June, 1837, a report was presented to the Chamber of Peers, by a committee of their own body which had been appointed to examine a petition from the manufacturers of Mulhausen; and the Chamber thereupon referred the petition to the Minister of Commerce. Mr. Martin du Nord, then minister, lost no time in drawing up a series of questions, for the purpose of collecting information, relative to the condition of the manufacturing population, upon which legislative interference could be founded; and these questions were sent to every chamber of commerce throughout the kingdom, accompanied by a letter from the minister himself,

* In Alsace (Département du Haut-Rhin), N.W. of Basle.

dated the 31st of July, 1837. This letter contained the following passages : —

" To subject children to premature and long continued labour may be productive of serious evils at that period of life; not only as checking the developement of their physical powers, but because it must frequently stand in the way of their education, by their not having the time necessary for it at their disposal. The consequence of which is, that many of them grew up unable to read and write, and feeble in body and mind; but well imbued, at an early age, with vicious propensities, acquired from their older associates in the factories. It is therefore a matter of the greatest moment to ascertain, with correctness, what the present condition of the children employed in manufactures really is, and I can apply to none with more propriety than to you, gentlemen, to enlighten me on this subject. I cannot too strongly impress upon you the duty of replying to the series of questions I now transmit to you, with that fidelity which I have a right to expect from men who, themselves receiving a just measure of the solicitude of the government, ought to lay aside every consideration of private interest that can in any manner interfere with a true statement of facts. In thus addressing you, gentlemen, I have but one object, which is, that I may know the moral and physical condition of the children employed in our great manufacturing establishments."

Before the end of the year 1837, the answers which were received from the different chambers of commerce* were put into the hands of M. Delambre, the

* The returns contained observations from the " *Chambres de Commerce*," the " *Chambres Consultatives*," and the " *Conseils de Prud'hommes*." The *Chambres Consultatives* are established in the manufacturing towns, where there are no chambers of commerce: they are composed of manufacturers, who are consulted on questions relating to manufactures. The *Conseil de Prud'-hommes* is a species of jury, who draw up general regulations for the internal concerns of the manufactory or work, for the settlement of the conditions to be observed between the master and his

head of the department of manufactures in the office
of the Minister of Commerce, who drew up a general
report, addressed to the minister, containing an
analysis of the answers. M. Delambre* was so good
as to send me a copy of this report; and the following
is a summary of its contents.

*Report on the Answers to the Questions contained in
the Circular Letter of the Minister of Commerce
of the 31st of July, 1837, relative to the Employment of Children in Factories.*

" It is to be regretted that many of the Chambers and
Councils have not yet replied to the circular letter which
was addressed to them; for although their answers might
not have thrown any new light upon the points which have
been made out from a variety of facts derived from other
sources, still they might have served to confirm the allega-
tions and opinions that others have stated. In this analysis
I shall follow the order of the circular, first in showing

---

work-people. It is composed one half of masters, and one half of
overlookers (*contre-maîtres.*) We have nothing analogous to it
in this country: it is very much to be wished that there were
such councils in all our manufacturing towns; for they might
bring about a better feeling between the employer and the employed than now exists; and might prevent strikes that too often
arise from a want of a right understanding between the master
and the work-people.

It is not easy to translate the term, but as the council is composed of persons of experience, perhaps " Council of Elders " is
not inappropriate.

* M. Delambre has all along taken a very warm interest in this
question of the regulation of infant labour. I had a letter from
him in September, 1838, asking for minute information as to the
working of our Factory Act.

the actual state of matters, and then what alterations have appeared to be practicable."

1. *At how early an age are children employed in the factories?*

" As early as *six* in some places, and *seven* in others, but *eight* and *nine* are the usual ages when they first begin. It is stated in the answer from Elbeuf*, that the profligate lives led by some fathers is the cause of many children being thus prematurely sent to work; and it is remarked upon this in the report, ' If that opinion be correct, the labour of the children serves very frequently to encourage the misconduct of fathers.' "

2. *What wages do the children receive?*

" From 25 to 75 centimes a day (equal to about $2\frac{1}{2}d.$ to $7\frac{1}{2}d.$), being generally in proportion to the age and skill of the child; but those of six and seven seldom get more than from 25 to 30 centimes. In those places where they do not usually employ them younger than eight or nine, they give them usually 40 centimes. At Dortan †, where they pay from 35 to 75, such children as are bound to remain for several years are also lodged and fed."

3. *What is the saving to the manufacturer in employing children rather than adults?*

" The greater number of the answers state that there is a real economy, from 30 to 50 per cent. Some, however, deny that there is any; because, in their opinion, as much is lost by bad work as is gained by lower wages; others say that if the children are young, the spinner must generally have two instead of one, and he would not pay more for an adult. Thus in the department of the Aisne, where that opinion is maintained, they would be inclined to discharge the children on the first change of the existing system.

---

* In Normandy, S. of Rouen; one of the principal seats of the woollen manufacture in France.

† Département de l'Ain.

" All concur in stating that there are certain processes which can only be well and easily performed by children; and that, at whatever cost, they must necessarily be preferred to adults; that, besides, it is an advantage to their fathers for whom they work, and that it is a way of rearing future good and skilful operatives. On the question of saving, the report of the Chamber of Commerce of Rouen contains the following remark : —

" It has been stated to us by one of our best spinners, who produces about 3000 lbs. of cotton twist a week, that out of 130 workers he employs, there are forty-two children from eight to fifteen years of age. So that, supposing that two thirds of these forty-two are from eight to twelve, and if they were to be replaced by others from thirteen to fifteen years of age, there would be a loss to the spinner of 56 francs a week, or 2912 francs a year, or an addition of $1\frac{3}{4}$ centime per lb. to the cost of his twist. The addition would be still greater if the scarcity of older hands caused an advance of wages; it is true that their work would be better, and consequently the produce would be more valuable."

4. *How many hours do they work?*

" From *twelve* to *sixteen :* the actual working is from twelve to fourteen, because, in general, an hour and a half or two hours are allowed for meals. The Council of Elders of Rouen say that it is too much; especially in those places where the children live from half a mile to two miles from the factory, which is often the case in the departments of the Lower Seine and the Upper Rhine. They say that the work of the children is not laborious or irksome; that may be true, but they admit, at the same time, that passing so many hours in the dense atmosphere of the factories is very hurtful. That is of course modified by the circumstances of the building. They add, that it must be remembered that the children would breathe a worse atmosphere at home: of that there is, perhaps, no doubt, but the child would not, in all probability, be kept fourteen or sixteen hours at home, without getting into the fresh air, which is precisely what he loses by being kept at work; and, on the other hand, if it be true that he quits a pestilential atmosphere at home to go into another that is unwholesome, so much the more is it to be desired that his stay in the factory should not be prolonged beyond a reasonable time."

5. *Are they employed during the night?*

" In general they are not; but it is not unusual in the chief centres of manufacture for them to work all Saturday night and Sunday morning. When trade is very brisk, they employ a second set, one set working all the week in the daytime, and the other in the night, alternately; but this seldom happens. ' But on such occasions,' observes the Council of Elbeuf, ' the means of production, that is, the exertions of the work-people, are strained as much as possible, and more so than is consistent with humanity, either by increasing the number of the hours of work, or by working the whole night. Night-work, in the opinion of all, gives the opportunity, or rather is the cause, of great demoralisation."

6. *Do the children of both sexes work together?*

" They do; but it is said that there always is a strict superintendence. It is admitted that it is injurious to morals, but that it would be impossible, or extremely difficult, to do otherwise."

7. *Are they in general the children of the work-people in the factory, and in what proportion?*

" The proportion varies from a tenth to a half, but the usual proportion is a third. They do not always work as piecers to their fathers: in several places the fathers prefer their working for others, and sometimes they work in different factories. In some situations, a father designedly sends his children to another factory, in order that if the one where he himself is employed should stop, the whole family may not be out of work at one time. Under any circumstances, the operatives will not be pleased with a restriction, either as to the age or hours of work of the children, because the result must be a reduction in the wages of the family."

8. *What is the amount of their education? do they attend school? and do they attend day, evening, or Sunday Schools?*

" The answers are unanimous in declaring that where the children are employed as early as six years, there is no education at all; for the obvious reason, that they have had no opportunity of attending school; that, in general, the children are only found able to read and write, and even then imperfectly, when they begin to work about ten or eleven years of age; and that it frequently happens that there is so much indifference on the part of parents in this matter, that many of them do not avail themselves of the Infants' Schools, or other establishments of education, generally gratuitous, which are now to be found in all the great seats of manufacture."

9. *What is the state of morals among these children?*

" In the lowest possible state: much to be done every where on this head; and it is a most important fact to notice, that the demoralisation of the children seems to be the greatest in those places where they are most early admitted to work in the factories. It is declared, that in the department of the Isère, the state of immorality cannot be exceeded. But this immoral condition of the children is not to be set down to the evils of the present factory system alone; many causes contribute, among which the profligate conduct of the parents is conspicuous in many places."

10. *Are the children ill-used by the masters, or by those for whom they work?*

" No; and much less so than formerly: and when it does occur, it is more frequently by a father or brother than by a stranger."

The object of the preceding questions was to elicit the present condition of the factory children; those which follow were for the purpose of collecting opinions as to the best practical remedies that can be applied to the evils that exist. It is observed in the Report, that when the Chambers of Commerce, and Councils of Elders, have to give statements as to facts which come every day under their observation, their replies are to a certain extent precise, and capable of being clearly understood; but that it is very different when they come to suggest changes and innovations. They put forth their ideas very vaguely and doubtingly, afraid to change even that which is admitted to be bad. They are, in this case as on all other occasions, the partisans of the maxim, " Leave things as they are ; " and among those who are most earnest for alterations, there is great uncertainty as to the means by which they would have them brought about.

1. *At what age ought children to be admitted to work in factories ?*

" The opinions are divided between *nine* and *ten*. All agree that the labour of children is indispensable for carrying on various branches of the manufacture : the work they have to do requires a delicacy in the fingers to unite the broken threads, and a suppleness of body to creep under and pass between different parts of the machinery, which do not exist in more advanced life. Independently, therefore, of considerations of economy, children cannot be dispensed with. If nine years were taken as the minimum, it would not occasion any very great change in the larger proportion of the manufacturing districts.* It appears to be the general opinion, that, in esta-

---

* The following observation in the Report, respecting Infants' Schools, is well deserving the serious consideration of those who know and feel the necessity of great exertions being made without more loss of time, to improve the moral condition of our working population : —

" This is perhaps a proper place for pointing out the advantages,

blishments with machinery moved by steam or water power, children may be admitted at nine years of age, *provided they shall have already been three years at school.* All those who are disposed to fix this earlier age of admissibility to work, are unanimous in recommending this last condition ; in order that the time during which they are restricted from working may be turned to good account in educating them."

2. *Ought the hours of work to be gradually lengthened as the age of the child advances?*

" The answers to this question are very various. Some say that it is impossible, others that it is very desirable it should be so, but that they do not see how it is to be accomplished.*

---

and especially to the working classes, of Infants' Schools. They afford to children, hitherto neglected, a protection from injuries, and the rudiments of moral training which they cannot meet with either at home, or in the workshops to which their parents take them. The benefits of these establishments appear, from the observations of the Council of Elders at Rouen, to have been duly appreciated by the working people there, who, from having been in the habit of employing their children at the earliest possible age, have begun to send them to the Infants' School rather than to the workshop. In proof of this the following fact is stated : — ' Among the weavers, children used to be employed as early as four and five years of age, as assistants to the weaver, who himself is often a child of ten or twelve. But since the opening of the Infants' Schools in Rouen, they do not employ children so young, and have found means of doing without them.' From this fact it seems fair to infer, that when parents take their children with them to factories, or other employments, it frequently happens that it is less for the sake of the wages they earn, than for the advantages of keeping them under their own eye, rather than commit them to the care of a neighbour, where they would have nothing to occupy them ; and that many a workman, in places where Infants' Schools already exist, or may be established, will gladly take his children there, and will in no degree regret the restriction which the law may impose as to the age at which they can be allowed to work."

* Theoretically it appears just and desirable, but practically I

Those who pronounce it to be impossible found their opinion on this, that in a manufacturing establishment, where the moving power is steam or water, all the operations go together, and are mutually dependent, and that it is impossible to limit the labour of the child, without at the same time limiting the labour of the workman who employs him. It appears, however, to be a common opinion, that from the way in which such works are carried on in France, too complicated a scale of graduation would undoubtedly render the employment of children and young persons impossible in spinning mills; but that two classifications, reasonably settled, are indispensable, and these it would be very easy to adopt,

---

believe it to be impossible, without opening the door to evasions of all legislative restriction of the labour of children, which it would be impossible to check. When there was no restriction, a boy began as a learner without wages, got very little at first, but these gradually increased with his skill and years ; so that the advance to the wages of the adolescent was gradual. But when children are employed by relays, when the adult workman must have two piecers in place of one, each working six hours, he must divide the sum paid for the twelve hours' work between them ; and it may be either in equal or unequal proportions. As the law does not allow a child to work full time until he is thirteen years of age, if a piecer who is thirteen gets six shillings a week, one of ten, and one who wants some days of thirteen, may have only the same sum, or three shillings. Hence the great temptation to parents to get their children passed for thirteen ; a temptation to which the children themselves are by no means insensible ; for there is this addition in their case, that, when they are allowed to work full time, they hold their heads higher in the factory, as being no longer in a state of pupilage. This is the great cause of the evasion of the law in this particular ; and the force of the temptation seems not to have been duly appreciated, otherwise it would have been better provided for in the present act. In an amending act it will be of the utmost consequence to take care that the power of evading that part of the law which provides how the ages of the children are to be determined, should be guarded against by every check that is practically possible. — L. H.

as is the case in England, provided that the restriction be general and obligatory; that is, to restrict the hours of work within certain limits, for all between nine and thirteen; and to fix other limits for the hours of work of all between thirteen and eighteen years of age. The Chamber of Commerce of Mulhausen recommend that children, from eight to ten years, should not work more than nine hours a day; and that those between ten and sixteen should be limited to twelve hours a day, and seventy-two hours a week, and they urge that all working on Sunday should be strictly forbidden."

3. *Ought it to be a requisite condition that the physical strength of the child shall correspond with its age; and that his constitution shall be declared to be sufficiently good to enable him to bear the labour?*

"This is said to be unnecessary, as it is the interest of the master to exclude children who are incapable of working well. It does not appear to have been sufficiently attended to; but the question is applicable, not to masters alone, but to parents, who, either from poverty, recklessness, or avarice, take along with them into the factories children whom the master sometimes only admits because the father works for him. With regard to the masters, it must be admitted that many pay little attention to the matter; but in many places a medical certificate is required. If such an enactment, borrowed from the English law*, were to be adopted in France,

---

* Our law has been here misunderstood in this respect. The absence of every thing like a systematic registration of births, when the Factory Act passed, made it necessary that some other expedient for determining the age should be resorted to; and no other seemed better, or more readily available, than the opinion of a surgeon, who should attest the child to have "the ordinary strength and appearance" of a child of the age certified. Had the spirit of the law been at all times faithfully observed, this substitute would have been a sufficient protection against fraud in most cases. The abuses have arisen in a great degree from de-

it ought not to be so until after the most serious consideration of the subject, nor without laying before the different councils the difficulties that have attended it in England, the abuses to which it has given rise there, the falsehoods which it has engendered, and which have led those who condemn the English law to say that it is a law of perjury."

4. *At what age ought an adolescent* to be allowed to make an agreement as to his hours of work, either by himself or by his parents or guardians?*

" The most general answer is, at fifteen years of age, with the consent of those on whom he is dependent."

5. *Ought night-work to be prohibited in the case of children and adolescents?*

" Certainly, for the threefold reasons of health, morals, and education; but in those situations where the necessities of the work-people are sometimes great, it is proposed that night-work should be prohibited to all under fifteen years of age, but that it should be allowable according to circumstances, and with the consent of the local authorities, provided it appear that those above fifteen only are to be employed, and that they shall not have worked during the day; and that permission for this purpose should never be granted for more than twice a week."

6. *Ought the children to be required to attend school?*

" From what is contained in the answers to former questions, it appears that, from every or almost every part of France, in urging that children should not be admitted to

fects in the Act, which contains little or no check upon the conduct of a surgeon. So far as regards children above thirteen, nothing more is required by the law than the production of a proof of the young person being above thirteen. The proof that has been almost universally resorted to is a medical certificate, the same as that prescribed for children under thirteen.— L. H.

* By adolescent is understood a young person between thirteen and eighteen years of age.

work in factories before the completion of their ninth year, it is not alone the question of their health that has been taken into account, but even still more that of their education ; for on this last point, it must be acknowledged that there exists, in some degree, an unanimity in the answers. It is recommended that parents should be obliged to send their children to school; and an earnest desire is shown to improve, by means of instruction and education*, the moral condition of that numerous class of young operatives, who bring with them, in general, into the factories, principles the most corrupt. Constraint is indispensable ; for custom and experience have proved that, unless education be rendered obligatory by an express law, unless admission to work in factories be denied to all those children who are unable to read and write, the object in view will only be imperfectly, and never completely, attained."

" It is no doubt very sad to be obliged to have recourse to coercive measures, to compel parents to give their children the advantages of education ; but unfortunately there are many, and they form the great majority, who neglect this duty. After all, as is well observed by the Chamber of Commerce of Mulhausen, this constraint will probably only be temporary ; but without it at present the schools, both public and private, will be little resorted to by the working classes. Three evening schools, for two hours, and a Sunday school, were established at Reims; the manufacturers sent all the children they employed to them, but very soon they were obliged to keep them at their work; for in place of going to school, they strayed about the town, and loitered away, in coming and going, all the time that had been given up for their education. In the department of the Upper Rhine some manufacturers, whose establishments were in situations where the means of education were insufficient, set up schools at their own expense. But they proved useful to those only who voluntarily sent their children to them ; and the indif-

---

* " *Par l'instruction et l'education*," two words very usually, but very erroneously, as we know by fatal experience, considered to be synonymous in our own country. — L. H.

ference of the parents on the subject deprived them of all means of enforcing attendance on those who kept away."

" The factory children in England are required to attend school ; why should it not also be the case in France ? The law may be more easily obeyed with us than it is in England, because schools in which the instruction is gratuitous are more widely diffused with us than they are there. The difficulties which were there supposed to be insurmountable have in part been overcome, and the same will be the case in France. We may rest assured that as it is immediate pecuniary considerations that now lead the greater number of parents to keep their children from school, in order that they may sooner get them into the factories, they will in future be just as anxious to send them to school, when they know that education is an indispensable preliminary to their being allowed to make money by the labour of their children."

" Ought children of nine years of age, who, by being able to read and write have got employment in factories, to be obliged to continue their attendance at school ? Little would be done for the children if they were not obliged, until they are thirteen years of age, to attend school for at least one or two hours daily, *besides their instruction on Sunday.* It is, in fact, from nine to twelve years of age that children in France are prepared for their religious instruction, which, of all the branches of instruction which belongs to their age, is that on which education, properly so called, mainly depends. From that must the child learn his duties, from that must he imbibe the principles of morality. In all the answers, the desire that the children should be religiously brought up is strongly expressed. Nothing will have been accomplished, or at least the work undertaken will be very imperfectly executed, so far as the moral training of the children is concerned, unless the obligation to attend school be extended to thirteen years of age."

The report concludes as follows :

" There remains one more question, to which little attention appears to have been paid, and consequently few answers to it have been received. *To what branches of industry ought the restrictions in the proposed law to apply?*

" It would seem to be the general idea that they should apply to those only where machinery, moved by steam or water power, is employed. But some of the answers would have them apply to allchildren, without any distinction as to the nature of the work, provided it be conducted on an extensive scale."

This report of M. Delambre was laid before the three general Councils of Commerce, Manufactures, and Agriculture, in January, 1838.* The report thereon, by the Council of Commerce, was the most explicit in insisting upon the necessity of adopting some legislative measure to regulate the labour of children in factories ; and they recommended a law nearly analagous to that of our Factory Act of 1833.

About the same time several benevolent individuals, by different works, roused the public attention to this question. Among these may be more particularly mentioned the publications of M. Gillet,

* The three " *Conseils Generaux*," of Commerce, Manufactures, and Agriculture, are composed of the principal merchants, of the principal manufacturers, and of persons of station who take an interest in agriculture. The Council of Commerce consists of about sixty members, that of Manufacturers of the same, and that of Agriculture of about thirty. Their meetings are held only occasionally, and often at long intervals, sometimes only once in two or three years ; when specially convened by the Minister of Commerce, for the purpose of giving their opinions on questions which he proposes to submit to them. Their meetings continue for some weeks. Their decisions are in no degree obligatory on the Minister. There is great difference of opinion as to the advantages derived from these councils, whose influence is not sufficiently exerted to render it very efficacious.

one of the mayors of Paris; several pamphlets by M. D. Legrand de Foudray, under a feigned name; some of the discourses of the Baron Charles Dupin; and the Report of Dr. Villermé to the Academy of Moral and Political Sciences (a branch of the Institute) on the Moral and Physical Condition of the Working Classes in France.

In 1838, as the government did not appear to be ready to propose to the Chambers those legislative measures which had been so urgently called for from so many quarters, M. François Delessert, in his place in the Chamber of Deputies, on the 28th of May, 1838, called upon the Minister of Commerce to declare what were his intentions on this question. On that occasion M. Delessert spoke as follows : —

" I now beg leave to call the attention of the Chamber to a question interesting in the highest degree to the welfare of the working classes, and to our manufacturing prosperity — the duration of the labour of children in the factories. It is a question which occupied for many years the attention of the parliament of England, which, after a very ample discussion, passed a law in 1833 that is now in full force. Nothing has yet been done in France, notwithstanding the numerous appeals that have come from many of the seats of manufacture. I know full well how delicate this question is — I know that the wants of the working classes, those of parents, to whom the earnings of their children, small though they be, are of importance, are opposed to measures that are called for, in order to afford protection to those same children, that they may not be oppressed by excess of labour; but I do not now come forward with any distinct proposition; I have felt it my duty to call your attention to the subject, to take advantage of the publicity of our proceedings, in order to rouse the attention of the country at large to the question; which, before long, must be submitted to your consideration. The Minister of Commerce issued a circular respecting it to the Chamber of

Commerce and the Council of Elders ; and their answers were submitted to the General Councils of Commerce and Manufacture, in their session of the present year. I wish to do no more now than to ask the Minister of Commerce, if it be his intention to follow up the investigation he has made on this question, which five years ago was satisfactorily solved in England ? "

M. MARTIN DU NORD, the Minister, replied, that it was a question of which he felt all the importance, that it was surrounded with many and great difficulties, that he was endeavouring to collect all the information he could to enable him to come to some practical conclusion; but that it would not be possible to take it into consideration in the Chamber before the following session.*

In 1839, the Minister of Commerce was too much occupied by political questions of great moment to allow him to bring forward any bill. Several petitions were again presented to both Chambers; imploring them, for the sake of humanity, for the sake of the manufacturing population, to take up the subject.

In the Chamber of Peers, on the 31st of May, and in the Chamber of Deputies, on the 15th of June, 1839, several members, among whom were the Count de Tascher, the Count Dubouchage, the Marquis de Laplace, and Messieurs Martin du Nord, and François Delessert, called upon the Minister of Commerce to give a definite answer. M. Cunin-Gridaine, then Minister, appeared by no means favourably inclined towards any law on the subject, but at last could not refuse to come under an engagement to bring forward some measure in the next session. In the Chamber

* Being in Paris in July, 1838, M. Martin du Nord expressed a wish to see me. I waited upon him accordingly, accompanied by M. François Delessert ; when he put many questions to me as to the practical operation of our law.—L. H.

of Peers, the Count de Tascher presented a petition
from the Protestant Society for the encouragement of
primary instruction, in which the petitioners implore
the attention of the Chamber to the abuses that have
crept into the factories in France, especially those for
spinning, where young children "are subject to labour alike destructive of their health and of their
moral and intellectual developement; for that while
so employed, they remain total strangers to education, and to every sentiment that characterises a
moral and religious being."

The Viscount Dubouchage said,

" The sufferings of these unfortunate children are frightful;
a fact which is demonstrated by the petitions that every year
have been presented. Many of the manufacturers of Lyons
have found it more economical to have their factories in the
country, where they employ children. As Dauphiny adjoins
Lyons, I am well acquainted with the facts. These unhappy
children, who live sometimes as much as two leagues from the
factory, have to walk there in winter through mud and snow;
they are worked fifteen and eighteen hours a day, including
the time for going and returning, and have therefore only six
hours of rest. Their condition is truly pitiable, and such an
abuse ought not to be allowed to exist any longer."

During the recess, the promoters of this measure
did not cease to urge it upon the attention of the
government; and M. Delessert observes to me,
that it is due to M. Villemain, the Minister of
Public instruction, to state, that he made every exertion in his power to get the Minister of Commerce
to hasten the preparation of the bill which he had
undertaken to bring forward. It was at last presented to the Chamber of Peers on the 11th of January, 1840; and was referred to a committee, con-

sisting of the Baron Charles Dupin, the Baron de
Gérando, the Marquis de Louvois, the Count de
Tascher, and Messieurs Cousin, de Gasparin, and
Rossi. The committee set about the task intrusted
to them with great earnestness : they collected together and examined every thing they could meet
with that had been written on the subject, either in
France or in other countries ; all the reports and laws
which had emanated from the British Parliament
relating to the labour of children ; the cabinet order
of the king of Prussia on the same subject, &c. They
moreover examined several of the most eminent and
respectable manufacturers from different parts of the
kingdom, that they might benefit by their practical
experience and intelligence. Having finished their
inquiry, they agreed upon a report ; which was drawn
up by the member of the committee the most fitted
to do justice to the subject, from his extensive knowledge in all that relates to commercial affairs and the
condition of the working classes, both in his own and
in other countries ; as well as from his successful
exertions on other occasions in the cause of humanity
and civilisation.

The following abstract of this report contains all
that relates to the leading points of the question : —

III. *Substance of the Report to the Chamber of
Peers, by the* Baron Charles Dupin, *in the name
of the Committee appointed to examine the Bill* * *relative to the Labour of Children in Factories.*

" We beg leave to render an account of our examination
of the Bill presented by the Government, for the purpose of

* I have translated the term "*projet de loi*" by our analogous
word " bill," and have in the same manner made use of our par-

protecting the children employed in the factories. No subject of greater importance could be submitted to the consideration of the friends of humanity."

" The vast competition that subsists among the individuals who in every country are engaged in the same branch of industry; the competition, no less formidable, among nations producing the same descriptions of manufacture, and struggling to obtain some advantage, are the most general causes of that fatal tendency in the present day to prolong, beyond all just bounds, the duration of daily labour."

" That disposition is excited by additional motives, and becomes more dangerous in those establishments where production depends on agents whose strength is inexhaustible, and insensible to fatigue ; such as the moving powers of water and steam. Thus, in manufactures, that progress which we admire so much on account of the ingenuity that has been displayed by the inventor, may lead to consequences the most fatal to health, and even to human life ; the workmen becoming, in some degree, sacrifices to the great impelling powers we derive from inanimate nature."

" If the immoderate thirst of gain leads some masters of manufacturing establishments to work their people to such an extent, that nature is no longer able to restore the strength lost in the labour expended by a full-grown and robust man, judge then what must be the degree of enfeeblement into which young persons, and especially children, must fall, when they are subjected to the same unmeasured daily toil? What must be the consequence of such over-work? rapidly declining health, diseases engendered by the occupation, premature and serious infirmities. Such of the younger operatives as do not become victims to this barbarity, arrive at manhood with broken constitutions and enervated powers, and afflicted with complaints which prove for the most part incurable."

---

liamentary phraseology, when it appeared to me most nearly to express the proceedings relative to the making of laws in the French chambers. — L. H.

" At the close of the last century, some benevolent individuals in England raised their voices in behalf of the poor children; they pointed out to the legislature those prudential measures which were urgently necessary to be adopted for the protection of the young persons of both sexes, so barbarously overworked by the owners of the vast steam-power factories. The first Act of Parliament which interposed a check to these abuses, is dated so far back as June, 1802. That date is very remarkable; for it was at that very time that, in consequence of the general peace, Great Britain was brought into competition with the other manufacturing countries of Europe. But England did not hesitate to step forward, even at that moment, to prevent the continuance of such excessive labour of children, and that too in the most considerable branches of her industry, the woollen and cotton manufactures; which, from that period, constituted the largest proportion of her exports. Experience has proved that in showing herself superior to the fears and menaces, and sophisms of a sordid cupidity, and following the dictates of humanity, England in no degree sacrificed the future prosperity of those branches of industry which she then subjected to restrictions. The increase of her exports of cottons and woollens between 1800 and 1839, in spite of the effects of the protection afforded by law to the children, has been 155 per cent. ; while in all other articles taken together, the increase has been only $11\frac{1}{2}$ per cent. As the number of her factories, employing machinery moved by inanimate power, has increased, the more has the necessity been felt of applying to all factories of that description these restrictive laws, which have been proved to be necessary for the protection of children and young persons, who might otherwise fall victims to excessive labour. If we draw a comparison of the exports from Great Britain of *all* her products, in the manufacture of which there exists a restriction on the labour of children, at the beginning of the century, and at the close of 1838, we find that the increase has been 102 per cent., while in other articles of her exports, to which the restriction does not apply, it has been 25 per cent. Thus, Great Britain, while she was the first to set an example of a protecting law for children and young persons, and took this step without waiting until rival countries would unite in such a measure, so far from finding that it has checked the progress of those branches of industry to which the restrictions were successively applied, has, on the contrary, seen them flourish and increase, with a rapidity four times as great as that of all her other manufactures."

" More recently, similar laws have been passed by two of the principal European powers, Prussia and Russia; and Austria has fixed a limit, below which children cannot be employed in factories. With these facts before us, of four great nations having anticipated us in the generous purpose of coming forward in aid of injured youths and children, we cannot, without dishonour turn a deaf ear to those demands that have been made upon us, on behalf of the young persons employed in our manufactures."

" In 1820 this subject was pointed out as deserving the most earnest consideration, in some of the inaugural addresses, at the commencement of the courses of lectures which were delivered for the purpose of teaching the application of science in manufactures. The Baron de Gérando, in his inaugural discourse at the *Conservatoire des Arts et Metiers*, said, ' We must inspire our children and young operatives with a love of reason, of order, and of exertion, and form in them early habits of active industry. Let us, however, beware of following the example of certain manufacturers in a neighbouring country, who, to glut their avaricious appetites, made unhappy children of eight and ten years of age work fourteen hours a day; a monstrous abuse, which did not cease until an indignant legislature instituted an inquiry, to show to what extent some sordid masters had taken advantage of the necessities of parents, and thus ruined in the bud the hopes of many a poor family.' These admonitions were not lost, they taught some of our mill owners to keep within such bounds as humanity would justify; but unhappily these salutary regulations have not been general, nor could they be so. That this has been the case, may be easily seen by referring to the work published by the noble peer who was the Chairman of your Committee*, and to the work drawn up by desire of the Academy of Moral and Political Science, for the purpose of ascertaining the physical and moral condition of the working classes in France; the author of which has stated nothing without having personally visited the seats of the cotton, woollen, linen, and silk manufactures.† When there exists, as has been clearly proved, so great a difference in the comparative condition of work people, even in districts immediately contiguous, what must be the result? Humane masters, who will not allow the children to be ill-used, are exposed to a direct and ruinous competition with their neighbours, who take an unworthy advantage of them, by the additional labour, pushed beyond all bounds, which they extort from the young workers."

" It is most gratifying on this occasion to be able to draw attention to the enlightened and generous efforts of some of the citizens of Mulhausen, a town self-created, almost in our own time, and which by the talents and exertions of its inhabitants has risen with a wonderful rapidity; a town where the daughters of the most wealthy of the manufacturers deem it a duty and a pleasure, to devote a portion of their time to the education of the female children of the working classes, and consider that, in so doing, they are maturing and completing their own education; a beautiful example of mutual instruction between opulence and indigence. The Industrial Society of Mulhausen, with the most praise-worthy perseverance, instituted an inquiry as to the measures which it would be most advisable for the legislature to adopt, in order to restrain within just limits the daily

* *Traité de la Bienfaisance Publique.* Par M. Le Baron de Gérando, 4 vols. 8vo. Paris, 1839.
† *Tableau de l'Etat Physique et Moral des Ouvriers employés dans les Manufactures de Coton, de Laine, et de Soie.* Par M. Le Dr. Villermé, 2 vols. 8vo. Paris, 1840.

labour of the children and young persons employed in those very manufactures which constitute the wealth of that town."*

" Remonstrances again and again brought forward, prizes offered, and petitions to both Chambers of the Legislature, have been attended with the hoped-for success. In the last session, two remarkable reports, the one presented to the Chamber of Peers, by the Count de Tascher, the other to the Chamber of Deputies, by M. Billaudel, upon petitions relating to the same object, gave rise to some debates of great interest, in which the Marquis de Laplace, the Viscount Dubouchage, and M. François Delessert spoke. The feeling

---

* We cannot, I fear, boast of any instances of so disinterested and enlightened a humanity in our own country ; but there is yet time to make up for past supineness and indifference. There is much, very much, still to do to improve the condition of our working classes, especially in the manufacturing districts, and to establish a better feeling between the employer and the employed. It is the employer who must begin ; he must give proof of a disinterested sympathy for those he employs. If such societies as that of Mulhausen were established in Manchester, Leeds, Nottingham, Glasgow, and the other great manufacturing towns, many of the sufferings of the working classes might be removed, and many of those that are inseparable from their condition might be immensely alleviated. There would be a rich harvest of kindly feelings towards those above them, of orderly conduct, of respect for property and education, and of willing obedience to the laws.

But if there do not exist *societies* of manufacturers to better the condition of their workpeople, there are not wanting, as I can testify from personal observation, numerous instances of the most enlightened, humane, and active exertions on the part of individuals, often with considerable pecuniary sacrifices to themselves. It would be invidious to name some and omit others ; and therefore I am obliged to deny myself the gratification I should otherwise have had, in showing by what really *is*, what factory employment *may be*, made by a kind master; by one who will give up a portion of his time and thoughts to the promotion of the welfare of those who work for him ; who are dependent in a great degree upon him ; and who would gladly look up to him as a friend and adviser, if he would only give them encouragement to do so.—L. H.

of both chambers was clearly manifested that the legislature should come forward as the guardian of the children. It was stated on the part of the government, that the interposition called for had, for several years, occupied their attention, and been a subject of their serious consideration; that the Chambers of Manufactures, and the Councils of Elders had been consulted, and, more recently, the General Councils of Agriculture, Commerce, and Manufactures; and in conclusion it was announced, that, in the following session effective measures should be proposed. The Bill, which is now before the Chamber, is the fulfilment of the solemn promise then made by the Government."

" The first thing to which the Chamber has to direct its earnest attention is the principle of the proposed law. It is not limited in its application to any particular branches of industry; the intended restrictions are not confined to those particular employments in which the abuses have been so often pointed out, and so undeniably proved to be too true; but it is proposed to extend them to every workshop and manufacturing establishment. But while the Bill extends its protecting enactments thus widely, it at the same time reduces the power of the legislature to fix what these enactments shall be, almost to nothing. It leaves the regulations by which protection is to be afforded to the children, in all that regards their labour, their health, their education, and their morals to be settled by royal ordinances, and even to departemental regulations, to be issued by the prefects. A minority of two of your committee maintained that principle in every case, in preference to the amendments which were unanimously agreed to by the rest. According to that minority, all that is necessary on the subject is a general law; in which all the conditions that it shall be imperative to observe shall apply equally to all descriptions of work; that no special restriction, either as to the age or the number of the hours of daily employment, ought to be fixed by the legislature; in a word, that the law ought to do no more than confide to the administrative bodies the establishment of such conditions as shall be sufficient for all branches of industry. We shall now state what the majority of the committee has resolved upon."

" We shall first advert to the grounds for bringing in the bill*, stated by the government, in which they undertake to explain and to defend the principle they have been guided by. They begin by observing, that the representations which have been made of the abuses existing in France are not free from a certain degree of exaggeration; that there appears to have been too great a degree of haste in drawing conclusions from the great enormities that existed in Great Britain, and the restrictive measures adopted there in consequence; and that it is therefore only to calm apprehensions, to anticipate possible abuses, that the government has been induced to bring forward this bill."

" After a scrupulous examination of the facts proved in regard to a certain number of factories of great extent, belonging to wealthy proprietors, and employing a large number of children, we affirm, on the testimony of eyewitnesses every way worthy of credit, that there are entire towns and districts in which certain descriptions of manufacture form the chief occupation of the people, where the age at which children are admitted, and the hours they are required to work, exceed those limits which ought in justice to be assigned to both. In 1837 a report was drawn up in the office of the Minister of Commerce, and distributed by him to the three General Councils of Agriculture, Manufactures, and Commerce, containing facts of the most deplorable kind; of children being employed at six and seven years of age, and of the extreme demoralisation in many of the manufacturing districts.† This report ought to have formed the ground-work of our deliberations on the measures proper to adopt for the protection of the children; measures to which the government called the attention of the above named General Councils, in their session which commenced on the 14th of December, 1837."

* *L'Exposé des Motifs.*

† This is the report of which I have given the substance, pp. 26. to 38.

The General Council of Agriculture appear to have taken least interest in the questions: their report is very much confined to the case of children being taken away from working in the fields to be shut up in the factories. They see no necessity for legislative interference; they would like to see mill-owners stimulated by honorary rewards; leaving abuses to be checked by local regulations. At the same time the Council proclaim, and justly so, the superiority of agricultural employments in supplying to the state the most sturdy defenders, the most sober and most laborious citizens, and those most submissive to the laws.

" Desirous of ascertaining the amount of difference in respect of strength and bodily vigour at the age of manhood, between individuals in those parts of France which are almost exclusively agricultural and those parts of it where manufactures chiefly prevail, the following table was drawn up:" —

Comparison between ten of the principal Manufacturing Departments and ten of those principally Agricultural.

Results compared.	Manufacturing Departments.	Agricultural Departments.
Number of inhabitants employed in trade, who are licensed * per 10,000 hectares † of territory - -	371 licensed	130 licensed
Principal sum paid for licences, for all descriptions of trade, per 10,000 hectares of territory - - -	9,917 francs	1,128 francs
Infirm or deformed persons ‡ unfit for military service, for every 10,000 young men fit for the service - -	9,930 rejected	4,029 rejected
Number of inhabitants necessary to supply an able-bodied soldier to the annual contingent	442 inhabitants	408 inhabitants

[See notes for above Table in opposite page.]

" Thus it appears from the above table, that in the same extent of territory the ten manufacturing departments give three times as many licensed tradesmen, and pay nine times as much for licences, as the ten departments which are chiefly agricultural. In addition to these results, there are other facts which we have collected from the latest proceedings of the Councils of Revision § in the recruiting service."

In 10,000 young men, capable of supporting the fatigues of military service, the ten agricultural departments give only 4029 infirm or deformed persons ; while the ten departments which are chiefly manufacturing give 9930 infirm or deformed persons. These numbers are *the averages* of the ten departments ; but we find

In the department of the Marne - 10,309 infirm or deformed.
In the department of the Lower
    Seine   -   -   -   - 11,990   —   —
In the department of the Eure - 14,451   —   —

---

* " *Habitans industriels patentés.*" All persons following a handicraft trade, or engaged in any description of commerce, must take out a licence before they can exercise their calling, and must pay the sum charged for the licence, which varies according to the particular branch of industry. This impost consists of two parts : 1st, the *principle*, which is the sum originally fixed when the tax was first imposed ; and, 2dly, the additions which have been made from time to time to the principal sum, for the purpose of raising a fund to meet certain charges connected with commerce.

† A hectare is equal to rather more than two English acres.

‡ When the young men of 20 years of age, liable by law to military service, are examined, those are exempted who have diseases or deformities which render them unfit, or are below a certain height.

§ These councils are composed one half of the military and one half of the civil authorities, the prefect of the department being the president. It is before this tribunal that all the young men of 20 years of age, liable by law to serve in the army, are one by one examined with the greatest care ; and they decide whether the person is fit or not. The proceedings of this council are very important, and are conducted with great impartiality.

Such immense disproportions ought not to be looked upon with indifference by the legislature; they are proofs of deep and grievous wounds; they show that there must be individual suffering of the most afflicting kind; they render the country weak in military powers, and poor in all the occupations of peace.* We should blush for the state of our agriculture if we could only rear for its operations so small a proportion of oxen and horses able to work, in comparison of so large a number of weak and mis-shapen animals.

" We differ with the Minister of Commerce in two points. In the first place, we are of opinion that there are some great and well known branches of manufacture in which the labour of children is carried to an extent that is greatly to be deplored; and for that reason we think that, in the first instance, and without more delay, a remedy should be applied to abuses proved most clearly to exist. In the second place, we are of opinion that those remedies, so far from being special and local, should be based upon an uniform principle, and that it belongs *to the legislature* to determine what they should be."

" We entertain none of those fears gently touched upon by the government in their 'grounds,' but pushed to an extreme length in the ' deliberations of the General Councils of Commerce and Manufactures,' of encroachments by the legislature upon parental authority."

The exercise of a pretended right of selling, without control or restraint, the strength, the health, the very lives of their children, we would have the law deny, brand, and chastise, in the persons of the parents, who show themselves unworthy of the name. We do not think that this end can

* " The fearful consequences that arise from excessive labour in childhood and youth may be judged of from the following facts: —In Normandy, for every 100 men strong enough to be passed as recruits for the army, there were rejected 170 young men of 20 years of age at Rouen, 200 at Elbeuf, and 500 at Bolbec, all manufacturing towns."— *Speech of the Baron Ch. Dupin, Moniteur of March* 7. 1840.

be accomplished by local and special regulations, transitory in their nature, and which may be revoked, and which would apply a restricted and tardy remedy to such offences — to such crimes. We must anticipate them by legislative enactments, which shall be general and permanent; which shall be at once provident and omnipotent.

" Were the law so general in its application as was proposed, were it to extend to all descriptions of work, and not be confined to factories and other great branches of industry, it would be almost impossible to frame enactments for the regulation of infant labour which would be equally applicable in the great variety of manufactories in which they are employed. It has appeared to us the preferable course to follow the example of that great and free nation which was the first to enter upon this career.

" We recommend that protection should be extended to all children employed, 1st, in factories, works and workshops for spinning, or for weaving or printing fabrics, whatever the raw material may be.

" 2dly, To all factories, works, and workshops, where the mechanical moving power is inanimate, such as water, steam, &c., because those kinds of moving power not requiring any rest to recover their strength, there is a tendency to continue the labour beyond what human powers can bear.

" 3dly, To all factories, works, and workshops, employing a continued heat, such as glass works, potteries, &c."

" In thus limiting the range of manufactures to which the law ought to apply, we propose, as we shall more particularly state hereafter, to confide to the wisdom of Government the care of applying the protective enactments to any other branch of industry in which it may afterwards appear to be called for."

" The manufacturers of all descriptions whom we have examined, men of great ability and experience, although they differ as to the measures they recommend for regulating the labour, appear to us to be of one opinion, that whatever measures are determined upon, they ought to be of general application; and that the same branch of industry should have no advantage in one locality more than in any other: they claim, in this respect, complete equality throughout the whole extent of the kingdom."

" It has been asserted, but erroneously, that in the different regions of France there is such a difference in climate and in the people, as to make it essentially necessary that the regulations as to the hours of work should be different. Such an opinion will not bear a serious examination. Our laws, founded on the experience of centuries, fix the same age for these capabilities which depend on the moral and physical powers. Whether it be in respect of moral responsibility, intellectual developement, military and naval service, or the schools of arts and manufactures, one and the same age is fixed for the youth of France, without any distinction as to place of birth or residence, whether it be in the centre, the north, south, east, or west of the kingdom."

" Another observation has struck us as remarkable. The bill distinctly admits uniformity as regards the labour of children in all manufactories ; that the law shall extend its protection to all children under sixteen throughout the kingdom. It appears, then, that the Government see no necessity for making any difference on account of varieties in physical strength dependent on race, climate, or territory, and in that view we concur; and we go still farther. Most assuredly, if it be necessary to fix by law the higher limit to which protection ought to be extended, it is a still more necessary, more moral, and more sacred duty to fix the lower limit, below which children ought not to be employed in daily and continuous labour. On this point we have endeavoured, by every means in our power, to profit by the experience both of France and of other countries. In England, the lowest age is nine by the law of 1833.* In Prussia, the same limits of nine and sixteen have been adopted for all descrip-

* Baron Dupin has overlooked the exception in favour of silk mills, in which no limit is fixed, and children are allowed to work 10 hours a day.

tions of manufacture. In Austria, children are admitted at eight. We propose that no children shall be admissible under eight years of age. We would have recommended nine, but for the fear of great inconvenience in the woollen factories, such as those at Elbeuf, Louviers, Rheims, and Sedan."

" Having fixed the limits as to age, we come next to consider those of the hours of work. Among none of the nations who are our rivals in manufactures is it permitted for young persons under sixteen to work, in ordinary cases, more than twelve out of the twenty-four hours. Those nations, however, might have been induced to exceed just limits, from the fear of allowing other nations who do not fix any limits to have an advantage over them. But so far from being stopped in her humane course by such sordid considerations, Prussia, which placed herself at the head of the commercial union of Germany, did not fear to establish a duration of labour even two hours a day less than the highest limit fixed by the English law. With such facts before us, we could not, we thought, under any pretext, propose a higher maximum than twelve hours, as determined on by the latter power. That limit, which is an hour less than that proposed by the General Council of Manufactures, is in accordance with the resolution passed by the General Council of Commerce. If that maximum of twelve hours' daily labour be thought enough for adolescents between thirteen and fifteen years of age, is it not evident that it must be far too high for children of ten, nine, and eight years?"

" Thirty-one years of experience have led the English to establish this essential difference, in fixing two limits to the hours of daily labour, the one of eight hours, applicable to children from nine to thirteen years of age, the other of twelve hours, applicable to those between thirteen and eighteen years. The General Council of Manufactures equally admit the principle of a different limit for children and young persons; but they propose that the limit of eight hours a day should apply only to children between seven and ten. Our proposition is that it should apply to those between eight and twelve, and to fix the higher limit for those between twelve and sixteen. The lower limit will also prove highly advantageous to the children in enabling them to continue their education and religious training. If there are any persons who think that in fixing those limits we have not gone far enough, we beg to refer them to the following comparative table :—

Aggregate of the Hours of Work in one Day, of seven Children, one of each Age of 9, 10, 11, 12, 13, 14, and 15.

By the English law - - -	68 hours.
By the Prussian law - - -	70 —
As proposed by the Committee of the Chamber of Peers - - -	72 —
As proposed by the General Council of Commerce - - - -	84 —
As proposed by the General Council of Manufactures - -	86 —

" We have adopted the middle term, because it appears to us to meet all the claims that can be tolerated on the part of manufacturers and capitalists. According to the above table, we give them two hours more than the Prussian, and four hours more than the English law. We cannot, therefore, be reproached with sacrificing the interests of the French manufacturers to those of foreign competitors."

"Another object of the highest importance is that of night-work, which in some places they are cruel enough to make continuous, even in the case of apprentices of nine, eight, and seven years of age. The English law protects, with a most praiseworthy severity, the young operatives against this evil, a species of work most dangerous both to health and morals; for it extends the protection to young persons of eighteen years of age. We have contented ourselves with proposing that habitual working in the night should not be allowed with young persons under sixteen, and that employing children under twelve years in the night should be absolutely prohibited. Finally, in extraordinary or sudden stoppages, in cases of vacations, or of repairing accidents, we would allow young persons between twelve and sixteen to work in the night, limiting it, however, to eight hours in the twenty-four. If the master prefers making up, during the day, time lost by stoppages, we would in that case allow an extra hour in the day until the lost time was made up, as is provided in the English law. We hope that having this alternative, mill-owners will, in almost every case, abandon the odious practice of working in the night."

" With regard to those works in which a fire must necessarily be kept up night and day, we require, in the name of humanity, that they shall not employ in the night any workers under sixteen years of age."

" We propose, as a positive enactment, that children and young persons shall not be allowed to work on the holydays prescribed by law. In the most tumultuary times of the revolution, even when we had the republican calendar, that right was given to the citizens of all ages. We do not concern ourselves with adults; but in framing a law for the protection of the health and morals of children, we propose that working on Sundays shall under no circumstances be permitted."

" Such, then, are the general enactments, which, in our opinion, it becomes the solemn duty of the legislature to prescribe, in order to protect children and young persons equally, from one end of the kingdom to the other."

" For the due enforcement of these measures, we would take the child under our protection from his first entrance into the factory, and would require that it shall not be lawful to employ him, without he shall have attended the primary schools for two years previously, or unless the manufacturers shall engage that he shall attend a school of the same kind. Certificates given to the children, and registers to be kept in each establishment, ought to show that the law has been strictly observed, or render it easy to discover infractions of it."

" Having carefully executed our functions as legislators, we have, with no less zeal, examined into the powers which may be intrusted with safety to the executive government. It is impossible that any law can provide for every case. We leave to be provided by royal ordinances, issued in the form of regulations by the executive, such general measures as may from time to time be deemed necessary; in the first place, to secure a return to, and a maintenance of, correct conduct and public decency in the places where the people work; and, in the second place, to provide for the continuance of the secular and religious instruction of the children. We may, on this subject, bring forward as an example the factories in the United States of America, where large numbers of young persons of both sexes are brought together, without the occurrence of any of that deplorable immorality which has called forth so many complaints relative to the factories in Alsace, Picardy, French Flanders, and especially in Normandy. If we take the nine chief manufacturing departments of these ancient provinces, and contrast them with the other departments, leaving Paris out of the calculation, we find that, for every 10,000 legitimate children, there are in these manufacturing departments, 949 bastards, in the others 383. This is the first proof we have to adduce indicative of the comparative state of morals. In a discourse that was drawn up for the purpose of showing the relations subsisting between morals, education, and manufactures, a comparison has been made between the *nineteen* richest and chief manufacturing departments, and the *sixty-nine* other departments; from which it appears, that in *the nineteen* there are so many persons engaged in factories, works, and trade, that they pay seventeen millions of francs for their trading licences; while *the sixty-nine* pay no more thirteen millions. But in *the nineteen* departments, the public prosecutions for crimes against the person have amounted to one for every 10,805 inhabitants, while in *the sixty-nine* they did not exceed one for every 13,137. In prosecutions for crimes against property, they have amounted, in *the nineteen* departments, to one for every 4792 inhabitants; while in *the sixty-nine*, they amounted to not more than one for every 8608. It appears, therefore, that in those parts of the kingdom where mechanical trades prevail, and which are the principal seats of manufactures, and in which large numbers of children are employed, it is become a matter of vital interest to bring back the working classes, by commencing with those of the most tender years, to principles of order and morality, to a respect for the security of persons and property, and to a reverence for the laws and for religion."

" The wer which it is proposed to confide to the government by ... two first enactments in article IV. of the bill, as amended by the committee, will lead directly, and we trust effectively, to that salutary result. Guided by the same spirit of affording protection to youth, we propose to confer upon government the power to pass ordinances, in the forms of public acts of the executive, for the following purposes: first, to prevent all habitual ill treatment and violent punishments of children; and, 2dly, to prevent those mischiefs which arise from the unhealthiness of the factories or of the employment; in a word, to guard against every thing calculated to injure the vigour and health of the children."

" In specifying, as we have done, in article I., the particular branches of industry to which the provisions of the law ought immediately to apply, we are very far from thinking that the range might not be usefully extended, either at present or hereafter. We propose to give government the power of extending the operation of the law, by public ordinances, to all descriptions of manufactures, works, and workshops, according as experience shall show the necessity of so doing."

" The general limits which we have proposed for the hours of work, and also for the ages of the young workers, may, in some descriptions of manufacture, be still beyond what is right, due regard being had to the health of the children and young persons. We recommend, therefore, that the government should be empowered to reduce the hours of work in all descriptions of employment; but that this must be done by a general measure, applicable to all parts of the kingdom, in order to avoid unfair competition between one part of the country and another."

" We approve of the penalties proposed in the bill, in cases

of infractions of the law, both as respects the masters of factories and the parents and guardians of the children. With
regard to the latter, however, we do not think they ought to
be liable either to fine or imprisonment, except in cases of
offences respecting the ages of the children. We would have
the same amount of penalty imposed for violations of those
parts of the law which fix the hours of work, in order to
put an end to this most blind, and most odious form of
cupidity."

" Subject to the direction of the Minister of Agriculture
and Commerce, the prefects, sub-prefects, and mayors, will
be intrusted with the enforcement of the law. The prefects
will therefore have to control and authenticate in each manufacturing establishment the hours of work, the intervals for
rest, and the different measures that are applicable to the
children. These various regulations, when so authenticated,
must be fixed up in the factory. We also propose that the
right of inspecting these establishments, and of prosecuting
for contraventions of the law, shall be given to the prefects,
sub-prefects, mayors, the king's procurators, and their substitutes, justices of the peace, and commissioners of police, with
power to call for the children, the certificates of the children,
and the registers concerning them. We further recommend
that they shall have the right of taking along with them a
medical officer, in order that they may satisfy themselves as
to the healthiness or otherwise of the factories, and of the
state of health of the children employed."

" From the extent of the details which we have thought it
necessary to submit to you, you will judge of the multiplicity
of facts, and the variety of evidence of experienced persons,
which it has been necessary for us to scrutinize and to com-
pare, in order to fulfil the task that was confided to us. We
trust that when you see the circumspection with which we
have proceeded in proposing the protective measures, how
little we have hesitated as to the necessity of imposing them,
and as to the urgency of interposing in behalf of children and
young persons, without compromising the fair and just interests, and the natural rights of masters and of parents, you

will give us credit for an earnest desire to prove ourselves worthy of your confidence; you will see that it has been our anxious wish to propose to the government no amendments on their bill, which were not justified by experience. It has been our desire to afford you the means of giving an additional proof to France of the deep and unceasing interest for her prosperity which animates you, when the question before you is the passing of a law tending to improve the condition of your fellow-citizens, and to render the lot of the working classes more happy, by providing for their health, their education, and their morals; in a word, when the object is to add to those physical, intellectual, and religious possessions, which constitute the welfare, honour, and prosperity of a wise and powerful nation. We trust that the bill now submitted to you will come out from that legislative ordeal through which it has to pass improved by the amendments which we have proposed, and by such others as will doubtless be suggested by subsequent examination and discussion."

IV. *A Brief Account of the Discussion in the Chamber of Peers, in passing the Projet de Loi.*

The above Report was presented to the Chamber on the 22d of February, 1840, and was taken into consideration a fortnight afterwards. In the interval, the subject was discussed in several of the newspapers; and, what was very remarkable and consolatory, all spirit of party was laid aside on this topic: the journals the most opposed to each other concurred in expressing a strong opinion, that it was the duty of the legislature to provide securities, that the children employed in the manufactories should not be exposed to excessive labour and other ill treatment.

A most animated and interesting discussion upon the bill took place in the Chamber, which began on the 4th of March*, and was continued during six successive sittings.

The first and part of the second day's debates were upon the general principles of the law, some denying that such a law was necessary, others that it was an encroachment on natural rights, and that no measure could be framed that would not be found unequal in its application, from the diversity of climate and other circumstances, in a country so extensive as France. The majority, however, maintained the justice and necessity of legislative interference for the protection of children, but considerable differences of opinion were expressed as to the mode ; how far it should be by the positive and special enactments of a law, or by regulations of the executive government issued under the authority of a more general law. The former was decided to be the most desirable course for the attainment of the object in view, to secure the greatest degree of uniformity throughout the kingdom, and prevent the executive government being swayed by partial views, that would favour one manufacturing district more than another. This being settled, they proceeded to the consideration of the several articles. The debates are fully given in the *Moniteur Universel*, from the 5th to the 11th of March. The following extracts will show the sentiments entertained by the principal speakers on the leading features of the measure : —

THE DUKE DE PRASLIN. " Some years ago, in this chamber, I had the honour to be named reporter of a committee appointed to inquire into the matter contained in a petition

* The same day that M. Thiers and the new administration took their seats for the first time on the ministerial benches.

from the factory owners of Mulhausen, a town essentially manufacturing; and, although the object of the law on which we are now engaged be to check or put restraints upon the cupidity of people engaged in trade, I must, on this occasion, do them the justice to say, that many of the merchants and manufacturers of Mulhausen, the proprietors of very considerable establishments, did themselves desire to adopt some very sensible measures to prevent children working more than eight hours a day, including their meal times; and, at their own expense, they set up schools in their factories for the education of the children. But these worthy men and true philanthropists were obliged to abandon their benevolent arrangements, for they could not induce others in the same trade to adopt them; and as the generality of the manufacturers worked the children four or five hours a day more than they did, they obtained a great advantage, so that the more humane persons would have been ruined by the competition. They presented a petition to this chamber, praying the government to pass a law to limit the ages and hours of work, and especially the latter. You see, therefore, that our manufacturers have been the first to ask for this law; and manufacturers in other parts of France have in like manner come forward in the cause of humanity and public morals." — " It has been urged as an objection, that England has passed eight different laws on this subject; but far from blaming England on that account, she has reason to be proud of having directed her attention eight times to this important subject. I have read these eight laws, and I declare that I do not find them in any degree contradictory the one of the other; on the contrary, the later laws seem to me to improve those that preceded them, on those points which experience proved to have been omissions or defects. I am of opinion, therefore, that the example of England, although in many respects the governments of the two countries differ, ought to be of great service to us, and that we should not allow ourselves to be outstripped by that country." — " I shall never believe that a measure dictated by humanity can be contrary to justice. I do not think that we can be considered as violating any right, when we are proceeding according to reason and humanity."

THE COUNT CHOLLET. — " Great exertions have been made to put an end to the traffic in black people, and most justly so; but ought we not to be quite as anxious to put down the traffic in white people? And can we otherwise designate that odious traffic so often carried on between unnatural parents and avaricious manufacturers, who extort from unhappy children a labour beyond their strength. I see no difference in the two descriptions of slave-trade than this — that in the one the slave is sold; in the other, he is let out for hire. And even in this last point of view, it may be affirmed that the children in many of our factories are less humanely treated than the black slaves are; for in the case of the latter, the master who employs them has a direct interest that they should grow up in health and strength; whereas the manufacturer, who only buys labour in the market, and pays for a certain amount, cares little for the health or strength of those who have it to sell."

THE BARON MOUNIER. — " There are two considerations in this case. The one is the danger to children employed in certain manufactures, arising from the unhealthiness of the places in which they work, or the dangerous nature of the processes in which they are employed; the other is the abuses that may take place by overworking the children in certain manufactories, in which the nature of the moving power causes a continuous labour, and therefore exposes, in a much greater degree, those who are employed to the danger of falling victims to excessive exertions. Now, in the last description of manufactories there are two descriptions of work-people : there are those who are arrived at that time of life when they have the requisite strength and that degree of experience which enables them to tell how much they can bear; there are, on the other hand, younger work-people, who cannot reason in that way, and who, from want of physical power and a sufficient degree of intelligence, become passive instruments in the hands of others, who abuse their power in the most cruel manner. It is this last class that stands in need of protection; it is them which this law has specially in view; and we ought to be grateful to those honourable men who have called for this interposition, and to the government who have not turned a deaf ear to their demands, but have required us to direct our attention to a law so interesting to all the friends of humanity." "As to what is said of encroachments on parental authority, I shall only observe, that it is not a question of restricting it; we are proposing only to restrict the labour of children who are not in a position to decide for themselves; it is a question of regulating the labour of feeble and defenceless beings." "The most lamentable consequence of this overworking of children is not the direct injury done to their health, for the humanity of manufacturers, we must hope, would put a stop to that, when such fatal consequences are apparent: but that which they can never put a stop to is the annihilation of all moral sentiment, which indeed has no chance of ever being developed. When a child, in place of enjoying the sports of youth, or looking around on the works of creation and of human contrivance — in place of his senses and his reason being thus gradually brought forth, is obliged to repeat the whole day the same mechanical motions, and after that toilsome work must seek the rest of which he stands so much in need; there remains not an instant for him to acquire those sentiments which properly belong to a man and a citizen."

After a considerable discussion as to the description of manufacture to which the law should apply, it was determined, by a great majority, that it should not have so extensive an application as was proposed in the Bill brought forward by the Government, but should be confined to manufactures for spinning, and for weaving and printing all fabrics, and to all factories and works where a mechanical moving power is used, or a continuous fire kept up.

The questions as to the lower limit of age, and the number of hours of work underwent a long discussion; no one proposed that children should be admitted into any description of manufacture under eight years of age, and a considerable proportion of the Peers who spoke were in favour of nine, but the majority adopted eight as recommended by the Committee. The recommendation that children from eight to twelve, should not work more than eight hours a day, nor between eight at night and five in the morning, and that those between twelve and sixteen should not work more than twelve hours a day, within the same limits, except in making up lost time, were agreed to. It was not proposed that the law should be made to apply in any manner to young persons above sixteen years of age. It will hardly be believed in this country, but it is nevertheless true, that it has been necessary to insert an article in this law absolutely prohibiting work on *Sunday*. The question gave rise to a long and animated debate, but, to the honour of the Chamber, there was an entire unanimity as to the necessity and propriety of preventing this desecration of the Sabbath; the discussion wholly turned upon the mode in which the clause should be framed. The clause as proposed by the Committee stood thus:—"No child, of any age, shall be employed on the sacred festivals prescribed by the law." To this an amendment was proposed by M. Cousin, the Minister of Public Instruction, who spoke as follows:—

" Gentlemen,—The Government cannot silently allow this clause to pass. You heard yesterday with what energy, and with what courage, the honourable author of the Report of the Committee maintained the principles of the law of 1814. I shall not be so weak as to disavow it. Yes, rest on the Sabbath is called for by the voice of humanity, of morality, and of religion; and I say this not only as a Peer of France, but as a minister of the crown; for the administration does but confer honour upon themselves in testifying respect for the religion of their country. The law of 1814 has never been repealed. But its due enforcement must be brought about by means very carefully considered, at a time, in an age, when indifference on religious subjects is unhappily so widely spread; when poverty is so prevalent; and when consequently infractions of the law regarding the day of rest are often excusable. But it would be much less excusable, were the Government, the guardians of the laws, to venture to violate them. I trust that, in every possible manner, and except in cases of urgent necessity, the new administration to which I have the honour to belong, will not set the example of violating, without reason, a law which is still in force. But if it be in force, why repeat it, as is done in the clause now under consideration? The repetition is, to say the least of it, unnecessary; but it may be injurious, by leaving it to be imagined, that, except for this particular case for which it has been revived, it has been formally abolished. I am inclined, therefore, not to agree to the clause as proposed by the Committee, however much I may be disposed to render justice to the motives by which it was dictated. Your Committee, no doubt, were of opinion, that if the law of 1814 be good, it is more particularly so in the case of children, as well for the sake of their bodies as for the interest of their souls; and they feared to rely only upon a law which is not now carried into practice; and for that reason they have proposed to revive it as respects the employment of children in manufactures. There is danger on both sides; on the one hand, of exposing children to the comparatively obsolete state of the law of 1814, in not specially applying it in their case; on the other, in thus renewing the law, of seeming to condemn it in all other cases. In these circumstances a middle course is open, by which both dangers may be avoided; by a modification of Article VI., which fixes the penalty that is to attach to all infractions of the law. At the end of that article, it might be added, that the same penalty shall be imposed for all violations of the law of 1814 with respect to children employed in manufactures. In this way the object will be accomplished, and at the same time the dangers I have pointed out will be prevented; an effective enforcement of the law will be obtained in the case which now interests us, without an implied repeal of it in others: it will rather keep people in mind that it is still in our statute book. I propose therefore that amendment."

THE MARQUIS LAPLACE. " The statement which has just been made by the Minister of Public Instruction, that the law of the 28th November 1814, is not fully carried into execution, contains nothing new to me. It is, however, a matter of very grave importance that such a statement should have been made by a Minister in his place in a legislative assembly: and, on what is it founded? on a greater demand for labour being called for by the present state of society, the Minister tells us; on the freedom of labour. Freedom! Let us, gentlemen, be on our guard against being constantly imposed upon by that sort of fascination which the term is apt to produce upon the strongest minds among us. We have, for a long time in this country, been apt to make a false application of this freedom, which acts as a weight upon us, and checks the truly liberal advancement of our institutions; we confound liberty, and an abuse of liberty, in many things. It is not necessary for me to say that true freedom is founded upon a just respect for those rules upon which a rightly organised state of society depends, and a complete, entire observance of them: if they are encroached upon, or any thing impedes their free operation, there is no longer freedom, but an abuse of freedom. Unfortunately in these times, we see among the industrious classes of society a general disregard both of the Sabbath and of religious festivals; and that it is a common custom to work on those days, in order to get another holiday, or to make more money. Do you think, that in thus allowing things to take their course, in making no exertion to direct attention to divine and social laws, so moral, so wise, so well calculated to promote the interest of all, we are advancing the cause of freedom? No, gentlemen, we are sanctioning licentiousness. In the history of all nations, from the earliest times to the date of our Convention, we find a day of rest in their calendar, following a period of labour. It is a natural law, imposed by the God of nature: man must rest after he has toiled; and as, in civilised society, labour necessarily brings along with it certain relations which are common, so ought there to be one common day of rest. The tradesman who keeps his shop open on a Sunday, obliges his neighbour to do the same, by the pressure of competition. He obliges that neighbour to work when he has need of repose, and at a time when the laws of his country give him an opportunity of repose. An arbitrary constraint is put upon him, an extra-legal constraint; this is not freedom, but the abuse of it. I congratulate, with my whole heart, the Committee, for having, among their other numerous amendments, framed a clause, which again enjoins, a strict observance of the Sabbath and sacred festivals, among our young manufacturing population. It was said yesterday, that this is a work of supererogation : no, gentlemen, as it is admitted that the law of 1814 is no longer observed, let us adopt the principle, in all its force, in the law which we are now framing : it is a principle eminently salutary for youth; and what will, I am sure, have great weight with you, it embodies a moral and religious sentiment, which it is well, and peculiarly appropriate to recognise in a law of this nature. I support, therefore, the clause as proposed by the Committee."

THE COUNT DE TASCHER. " We ask for the children that they shall rest on the Sabbath day; and we do so, not merely in consideration of their health, but of what is not less precious, their moral and religious instruction. This demand is moreover justified by the subsequent clauses in the Bill. According to the proposed Bill of the Government, and of the Committee, a duty is imposed upon the executive government to secure the secular and religious education of the children: how, then, could that duty be fulfilled, unless the children, by being relieved from work, had it in their power to attend to their religious duties, and receive the instruction of their pastors? I do not fear being deserted by the other members of the Committee in pressing for the adoption of our Clause, instead of the amendment of M. Cousin, in the efficacy of which I have no confidence."

The clause as recommended by the Committee was agreed to.

The important question of the education of the children occupied nearly the whole of one sitting of the Chamber : and some of the most eminent men in France, in the present day, among whom were M. COUSIN, the present Minister of Public Instruction ; M. VILLEMAIN, his predecessor; the venerable and enlightened BARON DE GERANDO; and the BARON CHARLES DUPIN, spoke upon the occasion.

THE BARON DE MOROGUES. " The third article in the Bill appears to me to require some modifications, in order to render it more effective. It very judiciously provides that the children must have attended the primary schools for two years before they can be admitted into the factories; but it then abandons all direction of their moral and intellectual culture, and gives them up to all the corruption that awaits them in the workshops. It leaves the continuance of their education, secular and religious, to arbitrary regulations; the hours of their attendance are to be fixed by their employer; and there is to be no security either that the children go or are sent. All these things are so urgent and important, that they ought to be provided for in the law itself. Ought it not to be rendered obligatory on the children to attend two hours at least every Sunday and holiday, and one hour at least in every working day? Even if to do this, it should be necessary to abridge their hours of work still more, nothing could be more beneficial to the country. The immorality in our manufacturing towns is something frightful; it is more than twice as great in our town than it is in our country popu-lation; and in some manufacturing towns is tenfold as great as exists in many of our districts which are chiefly agricultural. It is in these towns that pauperism is most prevalent, and where the public peace is least secure, because it is there that the immorality of the people and the contagion of bad example are greatest; it is there that some remedy for the evils is most incontestably necessary."

THE DUKE DE PRASLIN. "Education is extremely neglected in the manufacturing districts, for it is impossible that children under six years of age can have had the least instruction. Undoubtedly we must not, in our desire to have them educated, go to a mischievous excess, and interfere injuriously with their means of subsistence, or the welfare of their parents; but education is a nourishment as necessary for children as their ordinary food. I am of opinion that the education should be suited to the age and wants of the child, for, if pushed too far, it would do no good to him who is to be no more than a mere workman: still, however, he ought to be educated. I think the Committee have judged wisely in requiring that before children are allowed to work, they ought to give proof of having attended the primary schools for two years; or that those who propose to employ them shall engage to give them, during the day, the time necessary for their education."

M. COUSIN. " I wish to offer some observations on the two first clauses of this article; the first of which provides that, in order to be admitted into the manufactories, the children shall previously have attended the primary schools for two years; the second making an exception to that rule, in the case of those establishments where they shall engage that the children shall regularly attend a primary school.

" The age at which it is proposed that the children shall be admissible into the factories is eight; consequently, all children, to be allowed to derive benefit from their labour at eight years of age, must have commenced their school education at six. Does this, gentlemen, appear to you an obligation that it is reasonable to impose? The second clause, it is true, makes an exception; but it very frequently happens that factories are situated at some distance from towns or even villages. The consequence of which would be, in many cases, that the manufacturer must establish a school within his own premises. But that is imposing a very heavy burden upon manufacturers, and you also impose upon them a very delicate task,—that of superintending the school. I do not hesitate to say, that if you will look into the reports drawn up by M. Lenoir, and other learned economists, on the fulfilment of the English law,—reports which the Baron Dupin must be much better acquainted with than I am, you will find that the education clauses have proved one of the great difficulties that have stood in the way of the execution of the law. I fear that the same obligation, when added to so many others, will only have the effect of disgusting the manufacturers with the employment of children; for, we heard in the Committee very enlightened and very humane manufacturers declare, that if the law be made too stringent, they will employ no more children, for it will be cheaper to employ adults. This would be a very serious result, for the more indigent families would be unable to derive any assistance from the labour of their children. I intreat, therefore, that the Chamber will not lose sight of the practical view of the question.

" But, as Minister of Public Instruction, I must make some farther observations on the principle involved in these two clauses. They are so framed that the second is not an alleviation of the former, but rather a confirmation of it. The first declares that no child shall be admissible to work in a manufactory, if he shall not have previously attended school for two years; the second is not in the form of an exception to the first, but only says, that those who shall not have received that previous instruction shall pursue their education while they are employed in the manufactory. Thus, either before admission, or during their employment, education is obligatory upon them. This is neither more nor less than the principle of compulsion,—a principle celebrated in the history of popular education.

" If you will allow me to speak here in the character of a Professor, I will say, that there is no absolute principle in this matter; books of the greatest authority differ, the practice of the countries most advanced in civilisation differs, the practice of the best schools differs. In a word, I beseech the Chamber to give credit to my experience when I say, that it is by no means a simple question when a proposal is made to recognise by law the principle of compulsion. I am very far from being an enemy to it. I have seen it practised in Germany with success, and also in some of the democratic cantons of Switzerland; but I have also seen primary education flourishing equally well in Holland, where the principle of compulsion is unknown. It is in that country that primary schools have produced their genuine fruit; for they have made the Dutch people the most industrious and the most moral on the face of the earth. Therefore it is, I say, that we must not take this principle of compulsion to be an acknowledged general principle. That there is good in it, is true; I am not opposed to it; but it appears to me that it would be a rash step to adopt it as a principle in legislation; for it would be to suppose the question already solved, whilst it is still a subject of controversy.

" I regret, therefore, that the two first clauses in this article of the Bill propose the adoption of this principle. I will now state two objections to these clauses, to which the learned author of the Report of the Committee will doubtless reply; but which, at present, appear to me decisive. The one objection is more a question of form, but the other is one of principle. The proposal made to you is to establish the compulsory principle; now I ask you, whether it be in accordance with the prudence of a deliberative body to introduce so broad a principle by a way so narrow as a law relative to one special object. Speaking as a legislator, I protest against admitting into a special law a principle which goes beyond it; and which, if admitted in one case, must be recognised in many others, and become of general application. If you maintain that the children employed in manufactures should be subject to this principle of compulsion in the matter of education, what possible distinction, I would ask, can you draw between children employed in manufactures, and those employed in agriculture and other trades? The one class are not more objects of interest, are not more destitute of instruction than the others are: why, then, treat them differently? Consider well: if you once introduce the principle of compulsion in these two clauses of a law for a special object, it will no longer be subject to your control; for, either you will convict yourselves of inconsistency, or you must recognise it in other laws. Farther, if we had not a law on primary education, and if there were no difference of opinion on the principle of compulsion, I can well conceive that it might be wise and prudent to begin by applying it, having a view to its subsequent application in other cases: but we have already a law on primary education; and what does it say? Why just the reverse of what you are asked to do. In 1833, some very learned and profound discussions took place in both Chambers. These deliberations had been preceded in 1831 and 1832 by able reports presented by the Chamber of Deputies. Now, every one of these reports was adverse to the compulsory system; and in the debate which took place in this Chamber, the author of the report of your Committee, at the same time that he declared he was not opposed to the principle of compulsion, in the name of the Committee adopted the same conclusion which had been come to in the Bill presented to us by the king. The principle of compulsion was not adopted; both the Government and the Chambers preferred the principle of exhortation and persuasion. That being the state of the law, is it possible that you can desire to make education compulsory upon the children who are employed in the manufactories? Were you to do so, it would lead to this absurdity: that in a village, the mayor or the pastor, the two fathers of the parochial family, could not oblige any child in the village to attend the public school, founded and maintained by the parish and the state, presided over by a master who is a public functionary, whose commission is signed by the Minister of Public Instruction; while, in a factory, no child could work, without having previously attended a school for two years, or without attending a school while he is a worker in the factory: thus, there would be one law for manufacturing industry, and another for agricultural and all other descriptions of employment. Would not there be in that a palpable contradiction? and, in this land of equality, an inequality without either ground or reason? Remember, too, that constraint is not a good instrument of civilisation. The system of exhortation has this valuable advantage over that of compulsion; that it is more in accordance with the character of a school. A school ought to be a noble asylum, to which children will come and in which they will remain with pleasure; to which their parents will send them with goodwill: the principle of freedom ought to reign there, for confidence and love cannot be commanded; the cultivation of the human mind, to be truly moral, must be neither servile nor forced.

" It is besides essential that in all things the habits of the country ought to be especially kept in mind. Recollect that you are making a law for France, for a country in which there is no longer any predisposition to respect authority as such; in which any appearance of constraint would perhaps make the people avoid and even dislike that which in itself is good. People will yield to persuasion who will resist force. I have seen the compulsory system acknowledged in Prussia and in some parts of Switzerland; for we know that democracies make as little account of freedom as the most absolute monarchies; but it is unknown in Holland and in Scotland; and in France it has been tried but once; and in what times? Indeed it was not even then tried, it was only ostentatiously promulgated; and by whom? If I were to name its parentage, more would not be necessary to destroy the project of your Committee. Take good care, gentlemen, that you do not miss the very object at which you are aiming, in following the course into which they are proposing to lead you. You are well aware that already the primary schools are a heavy burden upon parishes where it is very necessary to spare the resources of the people as much as possible. If, besides that, you interfere both with the people and the manufactures, take care that you do not cause a reaction, which will not be long in manifesting itself; and that you do not produce a result very different from that which you expect.

"Is the honourable author of the Report aware of the results which, without any system of constraint, we have obtained since 1830? I say *we*; for these results are due to the talents and the zeal of the ministers who have been my predecessors, as well as to my colleagues in the General Council of Public Instruction, who, by their vigilance and stedfastness, have gradually brought them about. Since 1830, without compulsion, for the law forbad it as it does still forbid it, by building schools, by making manifest the utility and the honour that belong to them; and above all, by providing better teachers, we have drawn to them gradually an additional million of children, beyond what existed before the revolution of July. Yes, gentlemen, in 1829 there were attending the public and private primary schools 969,349 children only; whereas in 1837 there were 1,973,180. These numbers relate to boys only. In the girls' schools in 1837 there were 1,110,147, making a total of 3,083,327 children of both sexes attending school. Now the number of children between five and twelve years of age was 4,802,356; consequently, in 1837, there were only 1,719,029 children between these ages who did not attend the primary schools; and from that number is to be deducted that very considerable proportion of children who do not go to those schools, but are educated at home. This, gentlemen, is what has been accomplished in ten years; let us but advance at the same rate, and in ten years more, there will not be a child in this noble land which will not have received some education. Do not, then, despair of the good effects of a system of exhortation; and beware of having recourse, without any necessity, to measures which, however useful in appearance, are in reality dangerous, and, as you must have seen, wholly superfluous.

"I beg leave to move, therefore, that these two clauses be struck out, and that the third clause in the article under consideration be thus modified:—In place of saying that the masters of the factories shall enter in the certificate book the time that the child *shall have* attended the primary schools, which is imperative, I propose that he shall say, *may have* attended them, which will operate as a sort of premium on school attendance; for the young operative who can show that entry in his certificate book will be more readily engaged by other masters. This would be a reward or encouragement, but not an indispensable condition.

" It is provided by article IV., that public ordinances by the executive government shall determine certain things to be done; one of these is, to provide for the continuance of the secular and religious instruction of the children. I propose to omit the word *continuance*, because it supposes a previous attendance at school a necessary condition of getting employment in the factory. With the clause so altered, royal ordinances, maturely considered and adapted to the circumstances of the children and the manufacturers, will be a useful substitute for the two clauses which I propose to strike out. By that method of proceeding, which implies nothing sudden or violent, all the good expected from these clauses will gradually be attained. It *will be* accomplished, I say, and in a better way."

M. VILLEMAIN (*the immediate predecessor of M. Cousin, as Minister of Public Instruction*). " I shall briefly state the grounds of my dissent from what has just been said. The Minister of Public Instruction does not condemn the system of compulsion in primary instruction, neither does he approve of it : he leaves it as a question of theory, without, however, declaring that the application of the principle has been productive of evil. Now, I would observe, that in the case under consideration it is not a question of the principle of compulsion. The amendment proposed by the Committee has no object of laying down a principle, or of establishing a system; but it has doubtless appeared to the Committee to be proper, that the power which they have been called upon to confer should, as a matter of prudence, be accompanied by certain conditions. The legislature, as the special guardian of every one in the state who is a minor, and incompetent to take care of himself, might in strictness forbid altogether the premature employment of children in manufactures : but it does not forbid, it only regulates their labour. Thus, among other provisions, dictated by humanity, may it not reasonably stipulate, that a moral and religious education shall be secured for the child ? Do you see in that any imprudent establishment of a compulsory system in primary instruction? By no means: it is nothing more than a condition imposed by the law upon the exercise of a power conferred by the law. And for what purpose is it imposed? Because the power given to employ children may hold out a dangerous temptation to parents, and increase the chance of the neglect of all education, and of all moral training among the children of the poor. When a child remains under the parental roof, however humble it may be, provided an enlightened government shall have established a sufficient number of schools, that child will naturally be sent to school; it will benefit by the gratuitous instruction which the law provides, *and which he has time to avail himself of*. But when parents have it in their power to send their children to a factory from five o'clock in the morning, and to turn their little strength to profitable account, is it not possible that the desire of gain may be a motive with them to deprive them, as so much lost time, of that leisure which would enable them to obtain some useful instruction, and cultivate their young minds in some degree? Is it not then just that the law should interpose, and say : — 'You may send your child to the factory, but on this condition, that he shall not be stupified, and that some portion of his time shall be reserved for his education.' These considerations, I will venture to say, must satisfy the honourable peer who preceded me, that there is in this neither compulsion nor tyranny ; that it is nothing more than a precaution, and a reservation by the law, which is meant to prevent children from being employed in the same manner as adults. But it has been said that a precaution of this nature lowers education ; that to be honoured the school must be free. Consider, gentlemen, that while employed in the stupifying work and routine of the factory, this school, however humble, will to the child be a source of comfort, of relief, I might almost say of pleasure. Has not the poor child, after eight or ten hours' repetition of mechanical drudgery, need of some rest, when he may hear the name of God, listen to moral instruction, and have some moments of consciousness that he is an intelligent being? In that point of view, I consider the right claimed by the law, as proposed by the Committee, to be incontestable. It is not, as has just been said, to impose a constraint upon the child in addition to his work, but to oblige the manufacturer to show consideration for the living creatures he employs. For these reasons, and without reference to any ulterior amendments that may be proposed, I think it advisable to adopt the spirit of the clauses proposed by the Committee; that is, a conditional obligation that the child shall have received some education before he is admitted to work in the factory, or during the time he is so employed. There is in this no contradiction to a system of freedom, nor any implied obligation to make a compulsory attendance on school general: the ideas are totally distinct. In England it has never been proposed to introduce the principle of compulsion in their primary education; they do not oblige every child to attend the parish school; nevertheless, when the subject of the factories came to be considered, they imposed a condition, not upon the children, but upon the manufacturers, to prevent the young operatives they employ from being kept in a state of mere animal existence, and to secure to them some moral and intellectual change from the oppressive labour of the factory. It is only necessary to refer to two provisions in the bill of 1838, the one of which requires that the children shall be able to read and write, before they can be employed; the other, that they shall not be allowed to work except under the express condition that they shall attend school for at least two hours a day. Thus, gentlemen, you are not called upon to sanction a mere logical consequence, or a first application of the compulsory system; what you have to do is to provide some guarantee for the moral development of these children, whose tender frames you are desirous of protecting against the evils of excessive labour. You are invited only to imitate what is already put in practice by a wise and free people, where the freedom of labour is protected with a jealous care, and where the executive government does not exercise that constant control and power of interference which it may do under the sanction of our laws. On these grounds, I not only think that the clauses should be agreed to, but I thank the Committee for having proposed them."

THE BARON DE GERANDO. " It is unnecessary for us to justify ourselves in this place for the anxious solicitude we feel in the education of the children of the working classes. We know how warmly and with what unanimity that sentiment is responded to in this Chamber; and by those very individuals who are now proposing to modify this article in the Bill. This interesting discussion, so worthy of the noble character of this Chamber, is a sufficient proof of the anxious consideration it gives to every thing that concerns the well-being and the future destiny of our youthful population; and the deep and continued attention which has been bestowed on the proposals which we have submitted to you, is a reward for that conscientious zeal with which we executed the task that was confided to us. But in a question of such grave importance, it is proper that the Committee should lay before you the grounds upon which they have proceeded. That I will now endeavour to do as faithfully and as accurately as is in my power, trusting to you to make due allowance for the disadvantages I labour under, from the superior talents of those you have just heard.

" We put these questions to ourselves: Ought the law which is intended to afford protection to the children of the working classes, to be confined to the protection of the bodily health, or should it be extended to the moral health also? Ought it to be a safeguard only to the physical powers of the child without regard to the more noble, moral, and intellectual powers? Ought we to confine ourselves to the care of preparing a generation which will supply able soldiers to the Government; or ought we not also to keep in view the importance of preparing good and virtuous citizens for the state, and estimable men for society? These were the questions which we proposed for our consideration; and I now state openly and frankly that the ruling sentiment in the

Committee was, that our object should be to improve not only the physical condition, but also, and more especially, the moral condition of the children of the working classes.

" There are many things to be done to improve the moral condition of the working classes, but the first in point of order, that which will be most powerfully efficacious, unquestionably, is the improvement of education in that class of society. In that opinion I believe we have the unanimous concurrence of the Chamber; have we then failed in making ourselves rightly understood? Is the form by which we would give effect to that sentiment unsatisfactory to you? Show us a better, one that will guarantee more complete security, and we will cordially adopt it. But if you exclude our proposal, you will rob the law of that which, in our eyes, gives it most dignity, you will destroy its very soul; for we maintain that, upon that, all success in advancing the interests of the working classes must depend. The principle that we wished to embody in the law was this: that if the child, before being employed in the factory, has not received that instruction, and that religious, moral, and intellectual education which is suitable to the class of society to which it belongs, such an education should be either given or completed in the establishment. Such was our view. Would you prefer it, if it were so expressed in the law? I, for my part, should be quite satisfied, for I proposed that the principle should be embodied in these terms. But in the preparation of the Bill, on which we bestowed our utmost care, though we were not provided with all the documents we could have wished to consult, we thought it better to adhere as closely as possible to what we found in the law of 1833, which contains similar conditions. That law does not render preliminary education obligatory; but it is recommended by all the Chambers of Manufacture, as well as by the General Council of Manufacture and Commerce. In England, the education of the children must be continued for four years from the lowest limit of admission; the Councils of Commerce propose from two to three years; that of Elbeuf unanimously agreed to three years. We are told that the English law is not obeyed; this

I deny; it is so well obeyed that, as appears from reports recently made, it has been the means of sending an additional number of children to school to the amount of 100,000.* Nor is this all; for, what I consider far more important, at the same time that the education has been more widely diffused, it has been much improved in quality. And why has this been so? because a constant superintendence has been exercised over the schools. I will farther add, that, as has already been stated by the honourable author of our Report, your Committee called before them two eminent manufacturers who had just returned from a visit to England, and had seen the care with which the law of 1833 is carried into execution, and they stated to us that it is enforced with general assent. We had before us also the report of commissioners, eminent and enlightened men, sent by a foreign government, who remained six months in England solely for the purpose of studying the operation of the law of 1833. It is stated, at the conclusion of that report, that the principal mill-owners, relinquishing their former opinions, acknowledged themselves quite satisfied with the operation of the Act. That law, therefore, does not exist only in the statute book: and we rest our measure upon that example.

" But we are told that we wish to introduce the principle of compulsory education into the law; now as I have said that I will fully explain all our views, I will declare in the name of the Committee, that the idea of compulsion never once entered into our minds. I will go farther, and show, by reference to the Bill now in my hand, that compulsion forms no part of our plan: we have been represented as saying what we never did say. We have nowhere said that, when there is no school in the parish, the manufacturer shall be obliged to establish one on his premises, at his own expense. Let me in the first place observe, that Article IX. in the law of the 28th June 1833, renders it obligatory on all parishes

* The Baron has been misinformed here: I wish I could say that the addition was any thing approaching to the number here stated, or that the education "has been much improved in quality."—L. H.

to establish schools, and I believe that law is put in force. But it is said that, if the children have not attended school, the master manufacturer must set up a school for them : this is not the least necessary, for they would be sent to the parish school. I have visited factories in France, in Prussia, and elsewhere, and I never met with one established in a parish where there was no school. That may be the case in some countries where they are in arrear in that step of civil- isation, but no such thing exists in France. That is proved by the documents published by the General Councils.

" I will now advert to the more serious animadversion that has been made ; to the fear that has been expressed, that we are proposing to introduce into this law the principle of compulsion, which was excluded from the law of 1833. I will not discuss the general principle ; the distinguished individual who is at the head of the Ministry of Public In- truction, entertains the same opinion with myself, at least I hope he does, that it is a salutary principle. It exists in the United States, and in Switzerland, and I never heard any complaint of despotic rule, because parents are obliged to send their children to the primary schools. I could say much in favour of that principle : I could show that Article ccclxxxv. of the Civil Code imposes upon fathers of families the very obligation that we are now contending for, inasmuch as they are required to give their children the benefit of educa- tion. Again, it is said that we are introducing into the law a principle of inequality. Our opponents are so sincere men, their objections proceed from such a right motive, that I do not at all fear to meet them on this point. There is no inequality in the law we propose ; it is no more than a pro- vision for a special object ; it is not a general principle that we wish to establish, but we wish to provide for a special case ; and with your leave I will point out the principal reasons why children employed in factories form an exception, to meet which separate provisions must be made. Were we to proceed upon the general principle that throughout France all children must receive the same education, we should be led into gross absurdities. A man can neither be a nurseryman nor a farrier, unless he has had a special education for these trades; and there are a thousand situations in life for which a particular line of education, or other special condition, is requisite. No general rule can be laid down: all that can be said is, that when special circumstances require it special conditions must be made to meet them. Some of these I will now state, only repeating, indeed, what has been much better stated by many others in this Chamber.

" It is right to leave things to their natural course so long as there is no obstacle to impede it : we should never think of sending an engineer to examine the course of a river, unless something was obstructing its free passage. Now, what is the obstruction in this case ? Why, that their working prevents the children from receiving instruction, and is an excuse to those who will not give them any. Parents send their children to the factories, to derive profit from them : they find it more convenient to receive wages for their labour, than to pay for their schooling; and, thus, the parent and the manufacturer have a common interest. This is an obstruction that we wish to remove. We meet daily in the streets of Paris little children, called Savoyards, belonging for the most part to the Department of the Cantal, who are hired out for 50 francs (2l.), to persons who undertake to board them, for the purpose of being sent about as beggars. This is an instance of a cupidity which lowers human kind, and stifles all natural feelings. It is against such bad passions as these that we wish to obtain a guarantee.

" There is another class of special circumstances which I should wish to explain to you, and I shall have need of all your indulgence in order that I may be rightly understood. Human labour is composed of two elements, material power and intellectual power. Now, what is, and what must always be, the tendency of human industry? is it not this,— to endeavour to diminish the amount of the first element, the mechanical man, and to exercise that of the second, the intellectual man ? Assuming that principle to be admitted, what should be the effect of the invention and multiplication of machinery? Should it not evidently be to substitute a mechanical moving power for a human power; consequently, to take away from a great number of individuals the necessity of using their muscular powers, but conferring upon them, instead, the opportunity of a proportionate increase of intelligence? But, see what takes place in consequence of the progress of that manufacturing skill, about which we boast so much. To what does that extreme division of labour lead? Is it not that an individual, even of mature age, is occupied incessantly in the same operation, in the same motions? You have read in Adam Smith how many work-people are required to make a pin. How does it happen that the making of a pin should require so many hands? Because the same individual performs the same single operation every day of his life, from year's end to year's end; and is thereby condemned to a mechanical and monotonous existence. It is against that tendency that we wish to interpose some obstacle.

" In proportion as the discoveries in arts multiply, and as we make progress in improvement, in like proportion ought the moral and intellectual condition of the species to rise: the progress of civilisation does not depend alone on the increase of wealth; it chiefly depends upon the improved moral and intellectual condition of the population. All this has been often said, and much better said than I can pretend to do; but with your permission I will offer some observations which, perhaps, may not yet have been made.

" It is important to draw a distinction between an apprenticed child and an operative child; and I beg you to attend to the distinction I make. The apprentice is in a course of instruction; I do not say that he is taught all he has occasion to know, but nevertheless his faculties are exercised in a variety of ways; he learns the elements of a process, and by and by he becomes more skilful: in short, he learns a trade. With the operative child it is very different. I will take a very simple instance, from the very subject in which we are now engaged. A child, that has passed ten years of his life as a piecer in a spinning-mill, will have learned nothing; he will only have acquired the power of doing that which might be performed by a brute, for a tolerably docile ape might be taught to do as much. We desire therefore that the operative child, condemned to labour at a description of work that is calculated to reduce him to the condition of a brute, may have some compensation by receiving some moral and religious training.

" There is still another circumstance, to which reference has been made by those who have preceded me. The law confided in parents taking care of their offspring, that fathers and mothers would not withhold any of that care which their children require. But you take them away from their own fire-side, you take them to workshops among, perhaps, three hundred workmen. Will they meet there with those natural affections, that tender care, which are obligatory on parents, but not on their employer? On the latter there is no responsibility to take care of them. You withdraw them, therefore, from those who are their natural protectors. I could dwell long on this subject, but I should abuse your kindness in thus listening to me, and I will therefore sum up what I have to say in a very few words. So far from our proposal being an act of tyranny, we dare to say that no provision in the law is more humane, or more advantageous, either to the master or his work-people. We could read to you the very interesting testimony which we have received from one of the partners in one of the largest manufacturing establishments in France, one in which they employ from 1700 to 1800 people. He stated, that for the last twenty years he and his partners had turned their attention to the moral condition of their work-people, and that they had gradually succeeded in raising it; and that in the same progression the produce of their industry improved in quality and quantity. And in truth, gentlemen, there is no better auxiliary to labour than sound morals. Those are the best workmen who have upright and honest sentiments. Improve the moral condition of the working classes, and you will improve their worldly condition. You may make better provision for these objects than we have done—we hope you may; but we call upon you to sanction the principle by making it a part of the law."

M. BOURDEAU. — "I am well aware of the efforts which have been made by the Council of Public Instruction to diffuse primary instruction, and that their efforts have been crowned with great success; but we are still far from the point at which we are desirous of arriving. Undoubtedly, in those places where there is a dense population, primary instruction has advanced with rapid strides, and the people have flocked to the schools with eagerness and pleasure. But it is very different in the country. In the greater proportion of the rural districts some have no teachers, and in others the schools are so scattered that it is impossible for the children to attend them. As, for instance, in those parishes of three or four leagues area, where the school is established in the principal place, it is utterly impossible for the children in the distant villages to attend it, especially in winter, when the communication is so bad. I speak of what I have witnessed with my own eyes every year. With all the disposition in the world, on the part of the parents, to send their children to the place where they might receive some education, it is wholly out of their power to overcome the difficulties, arising from the state of the communications between their residences and the school. Under such circumstances, to prevent parents getting employment for their children in the manufactories unless they shall have attended school for two years previously, is asking the people to comply with a condition which it is physically impossible for them to do. Primary instruction is advancing but slowly. We must therefore give the people time to make the necessary preparations, and we must avoid the inconveniences of too hasty measures. I have therefore to propose, as an amendment, that this obligation of school attendance for two years before children can be admitted to the factories shall not take effect until the year 1846."

M. HUMBLOT-CONTÉ. — " The proposition is that children shall be admitted to work at eight years of age, if they shall have attended school for two years previously. Now, every one must see that, at so early a time of life, the children could make very little progress, and, unless their education be continued, they will very soon forget the little they had learned. They are to be admissible on the production of a certificate that they have attended a primary school for two years, without any proof that they have received any solid instruction calculated to do them any good; and the clause, as proposed by the Committee, is so worded, that a child, so admitted with a certificate, is not required to attend school any longer. By Article II. that has already been agreed to, the children will have a long interval of leisure every day, during which they will be left to themselves without any occupation. It appears to me a great defect, that no provision has been made as to what is to become of the children in that interval. They are usually employed along with their parents: they will, at the expiration of their limited time, be obliged to leave the factory: where are they to go to—who is to take care of them? Their parents, being at work in the factory, they will wander about, without any one to look after them. I think the Committee ought to have taken care that they should be required in that interval to go to a school, where they may receive religious instruction; for I maintain, that primary instruction produces little effect upon the morals of the working classes, unless it be at the same time accompanied by a serious religious education. Most assuredly, it will not be during the two years, from six to eight, that the children will be able to receive any religious and secular instruction that will do them much good. I say, therefore, that, having given the children leisure, they ought not to be lost sight of during that leisure; you ought to provide that it shall be well employed for their advantage. I shall not draw up any amendment, for nothing is so difficult in a matter surrounded as this is with difficulties; but if you wish your law to be effective, if it is at all to operate in rearing more moral citizens, you must take care that the intervals of leisure given to the children be usefully employed. I shall content myself with voting for the rejection of the clause which makes it obligatory on the children to have been two years at a primary school, where nine out of ten of them will have learned nothing."

After several other peers had spoken, the amendment of the Minister of Public Instruction was put to the vote, and agreed to.

The discussion of the other clauses of the Bill occupied two more days; and when they had been gone through, the adoption of the whole Bill, so amended, was put to the vote, and carried by a majority of 56; 91 voting for its adoption, and 35 for its rejection. The Bill was presented to the Chamber of Deputies on the 11th of April, by M. Gouin, the Minister of Commerce.

V. BILL *to regulate the Labour of Children* * *employed in Factories, Works, or Workshops* † *; as amended by* THE CHAMBER OF PEERS.

ARTICLE I. No child shall be employed in manufactories for the spinning, weaving, or printing of fabrics; or in manu-

---

* The term "*enfants*" is applied indiscriminately to all under sixteen years of age.

† The words are "*Manufactures, Usines, ou Ateliers.*"

The term ATELIER is generally applied to the buildings or places where the operatives work in common, without there being any great mechanical power: the shoemakers' *atelier*, the weavers' *atelier*, the blacksmiths' *atelier*.

FABRIQUE indicates something greater, a more extensive establishment, in which a much larger number of persons are employed than in an *atelier;* but in a *fabrique* there is not always steam or water power: thus, print works, porcelain works, potteries, are *fabriques*. It is difficult to point out the difference between *Manufacture* and *Fabrique*. The term *manufacture* is usually applied to very large establishments where there is much machinery employed. A cotton mill is usually called *Filature de Coton*, a woollen mill *Filature de Laine*, &c., a print work *Fabrique d'impression*.

USINES comprehend more particularly those establishments where they work in metals, and most generally where they are

factories, works, or workshops, where a mechanical moving power is used, or a continuous fire kept up, except in conformity with the provisions contained in the present law.

ARTICLE II. No child shall be admissible into the manufactories, specified in Article I, who shall not have completed his or her eighth year of age.

No child, between eight and twelve years of age, shall be employed in effective work for a longer time than eight hours in any one day; and these divided by an interval of rest.

No child, between twelve and sixteen years of age, shall be employed in effective work for a longer time than twelve hours in any one day; and these divided by intervals of rest.

The hours of work shall be between five o'clock in the morning and eight o'clock in the evening.

No child, of whatever age, shall be employed on any of the sacred festivals prescribed by law.*

In cases of working in the night, from sudden and extraordinary causes, by reason of stoppages of the moving power†, or urgent repairs, no child that is less than twelve years of age shall be employed, and those employed shall not work more than eight hours in the twenty-four.

In order to avoid the necessity of night-work, it shall be lawful for the manufacturer to work one hour longer in the day-time, provided he does not exceed the number of hours that were lost in the preceding month, by stoppages, accidents, and other extraordinary causes.

---

manufactured by means of fire and machinery, such as an iron foundry, copper works, lead works. Works where the fire-blast is produced by bellows worked by machinery, such as glass works, are also called *Usines*.

* "*Jours feriés.*" The days on which work ought to be suspended for religious duties, such as Sundays, and the great Christian festivals.

† "*Chômage d'un Moteur.*" The days of *chômage* are those on which work is suspended by causes to which the factory, &c. is liable, such as machinery going wrong, droughts, floods, &c.

In works in which a continuous fire must be kept up, and in which working in the night is indispensable, children above twelve years of age may be employed, provided their hours of work do not exceed eight in the twenty-four.

ARTICLE III. The masters of manufacturing establishments shall deliver to the father, mother, or guardian of every child, a certificate-book *, countersigned by the mayor, in which shall be inserted the christian and surname, place of birth, and residence of the child, the length of time he may have attended the primary schools, and the date of his admission to the factory.

Manufacturers shall also keep a special register, in which shall be entered all the particulars required by the preceding paragraph to be contained in the certificate-book of each child.

ARTICLE IV. In the case of all factories and works described in Article I., ordinances by the government † may be issued, according to the circumstances of the different descriptions of manufacture, prescribing such regulations as may be necessary : —

1. For the maintenance of good morals and public decency in workshops, works, and manufactures.
2. To secure the primary and religious instruction of the children.
3. To fix the hours of labour, that are indispensable on

---

* " Livret" is a small 8vo. register, which every workman is required by law to have, which is countersigned by the mayor of the district (commune), where the factory is situated, in which must be entered the date of his admission and of his leaving every workshop or factory where he has been employed. These certificate books, although required, are very often not asked for, both by workmen and managers.

† " Réglemens d'administration publique" are ordinances or regulations drawn up by a minister, discussed and approved of by the council of state, and confirmed by the signature of the King.

festival days, in those works where a continuous fire must be kept up.

4. To prevent all ill-usage or excessive punishments of the children.

5. To provide for the healthiness of the factories, and for the preservation of the health of the children.

ARTICLE V. Ordinances by the government may be issued :

1. To extend the provisions of the present law to other kinds of manufacture and works in which children are employed, besides those stated in Article I.

2. To raise the minimum of age, and reduce the number of hours of work specified in Article II., in those particular descriptions of manufacture, where it shall be proved, by experience, that the hours of work therein fixed are still excessive, due regard being had to the health and strength of the children.

3. To determine those descriptions of employment in which, either on account of their dangerous or unhealthy nature, children under sixteen years of age shall not be employed.

ARTICLE VI. The prefects, sub-prefects, and mayors are specially charged, subject to the direction of the Minister of Agriculture and Commerce, with the enforcement of the several provisions of order, inspection, and protection contained in the present law.

All the internal regulations of the establishments, specified in Article I., with regard to the hours of work, intervals of rest, and school attendance, as also night work, and all rules of discipline applicable to the children, must be approved of by the prefect, in order that they may be in conformity with the present law, and with the ordinances issued under its authority.

These regulations, when so approved of by the prefect, shall be fixed up in the interior of every workshop in which children are employed.

ARTICLE VII. Every infraction by owners or occupiers of factories, works, or workshops, either of the present law or of any ordinances of the executive government issued under the authority of the present law, shall be punished by a fine of not less than sixteen francs (13s. 4d.), and not exceeding 100 francs (4l.)*, which shall be doubled in cases of a repetition of the offence : all without prejudice to those pains and penalties which may be incurred by crimes and offences against, or contraventions of, any existing laws.

ARTICLE VIII. Parents and guardians who shall have allowed the violation of the provisions contained in Article II., by consenting to the employment of their children before they are of the age prescribed by the present law, or for a longer time than is allowed by the same article, shall be liable to a fine of not less than five (4s. 2d.), and not exceeding fifteen francs (12s. 6d.). In cases of a repetition of the offence, a punishment of three days' imprisonment may be pronounced against them.

ARTICLE IX. The prefects, sub-prefects, and mayors are authorised to visit, during the hours of work, all manufactories described in Article I., to ascertain whether there be any contravention of the provisions of the present law. For that purpose they may require the production of all registers, regulations, and certificates, and also of the children themselves. These magistrates may take along with them a physician, entrusted by the prefect with the duty, to judge of the healthiness of the factories, and of the condition of the children as to health.

ARTICLE X. The provisions of the present•law shall not take effect until the expiration of six months from its being promulgated.

The Bill has undergone several alterations in the Committee of the Chamber of Deputies; some of

---

* It was explained in the debate, that these sums apply to *each child* in the factory, so that the penalty increases with the number of children unlawfully employed, and does not, as in our present law, attach to the *description of offence* only.

which are improvements, but others the reverse, in so far as the efficiency of the law is concerned. The Report of the Committee, drawn up by M. Renouard, a member of the Court of Cassation, was presented to the Chamber on the 25th of May; but, on the 30th, it was resolved, that, as on account of the great pressure of business at the present advanced period of the session, there might not be time to examine the question with all the care it demands, it was better to postpone the discussion on the Report till the opening of the next session, in January, 1841.

VI. Law *in* Prussia, *for regulating the Labour of Children in Manufactories.*

I have not been able, as in the case of France, to obtain detailed information as to the moral and physical condition of the work-people employed in the manufactories of Prussia; but my own observ-ations, during a residence in the Rhenish Provinces from 1831 to 1833, before my attention had been particularly called to the subject, strongly impressed me with the belief of the necessity of some legislative interference, on behalf of the children. By the favour of Lord Palmerston, I have obtained from the Minister of the Interior, Herr von Rochow, authentic copies of the " Regulativ," or law, for regulating the employment of children and young persons, and of the Cabinet Order of the King, approving of the law. Herr von Rochow has farther been so very obliging as to send along with these documents a memorandum, drawn up by himself, dated the 14th of April, 1840, stating the reasons for the legislative interference in that country, and the principles on which the Regulations were framed. I have translated these documents entire, without abridgment.

REGULATIONS *for the Employment of the young Operatives in Manufactories.*

I. No child who shall not have completed his ninth year shall be employed in daily labour in any manufactory, or in the works attached to mines.

II. No one, who shall not have completed his sixteenth year, shall be employed in any of the before-mentioned works, unless he shall previously have received, during three years, regular school instruction, or shall prove, by a certificate from the school authorities, that he can read his mother tongue with fluency, and has made a beginning in learning to write.

No exception from this Regulation shall be allowed, unless the owner of the manufactory shall secure education to the young persons employed, by establishing and maintaining a school upon his premises. The judging of the fulfilment of this condition shall belong to the provincial governments, who, in this case, shall fix the proportion between the time for school and the time for work.

III. No young person who shall not have completed his sixteenth year shall be employed in any of the before-mentioned works for a longer time than ten hours in any one day.

But the local police magistrates are empowered to grant an extension of these hours of labour when the regular employment in the before-mentioned works shall have been interrupted, either by natural causes or by accidents, when a making up of time lost thereby is requisite. But this additional time shall not exceed one hour in any one day, nor be continued for a longer period than four weeks at most.

IV. During the hours of work fixed by the foregoing regulations, the operatives shall have an interval of a quarter of an hour's rest in the forenoon and the afternoon; and at noon, one entire hour besides; and on each of those occasions they shall have the opportunity of taking exercise in the open air.

V. All employment of the said young persons before five o'clock in the morning, or after nine o'clock at night, or upon Sundays, or upon sacred festival days, is expressly prohibited.

VI. Operatives belonging to any Christian sect, who shall not have yet received the Holy Sacrament, shall not be employed in any of the before-mentioned works during those hours set apart by their regular pastors for their instruction preparatory to their confirmation.

VII. The proprietors of the before-mentioned works, employing young persons therein, are ordered to keep an exact and full register of their names, ages, residences, parents, and of the date of their admission; to have the said register always in the factory; and, when required, to produce the same to the officers of police and to the school authorities.

VIII. Masters of the said works, or their authorised agents, who shall violate any of the preceding regulations, shall be punished by a penalty of not less than one, and not exceeding five thalers (*three to fifteen shillings*) for each child so illegally employed.

In case of the register prescribed by regulation VII. not having been made out or regularly kept, a penalty of not less than one, and not exceeding five thalers, shall be imposed for a first offence; for a second offence, the penalty shall not be less than five, and shall not exceed fifty thalers (7*l.* 10*s.*): and the local police authorities shall have the power, at any time, to cause the before-mentioned register to be made out or completed, at the expense of the party contravening the law; which expenses may be levied without further process, by the said authorities.

IX. The legal provisions respecting the duty of parents to send their children to school are in no respect changed by the preceding regulations. Nevertheless, the provincial governments shall take care, in the case of children employed in factories, who are of the ·age that imposes the necessity of attending school, that the hours for their attending school shall interfere as little as possible with the internal arrangements of the factory.

X. The Ministers for the regulation of Medical Affairs, of Police, and of Finance, are empowered to make such sanitory regulations, and such other regulations respecting the morals of the factory operatives, as shall be necessary for their health and moral character; and the penalties that may be imposed by such regulations shall not exceed fifty thalers, or a period of imprisonment corresponding to that rate of pecuniary fine.

Berlin, the 9th of March, 1839,

By the Ministers of State,

FREDERICK WILLIAM, Crown Prince.

Baron von Altenstein; von Kamptz; Mühler; von Rochow; von Nagler; Count von Alvensleben; Baron von Werther; von Rauch.

CABINET ORDER *of* THE KING, *approving of the above Regulations.*

The Regulations, consisting of ten paragraphs, respecting the employment of young operatives in factories, which have been submitted to me by the Report of the Ministers of State of the 9th of March, fulfil desires long since expressed by the States in the Rhenish Provinces.

I therefore hereby confirm them in every particular; declare them to have the force of law throughout every part of the monarchy; and direct the Ministers of State to make the said regulations and these presents public in the official Gazette of the Laws.

Berlin, the 6th of April, 1839,

To the Ministers of State.

FREDERICK WILLIAM.

REASONS *for the Law for regulating the Employment of young Operatives in Manufactures, contained in the Official Gazette of the Laws for the Kingdom of Prussia, No. 2005., dated the 9th of March,* 1839.

His Majesty, by a royal cabinet order of the 12th of May, 1828, was pleased to direct the attention of his ministers, the Barons von Altenstein and von Schuckmann to a report from Lieutenant General von Horn, that the manufacturing districts could not fully supply their contingents for the recruiting of the army, and that the agricultural districts had in part to make up the deficiency; and His Majesty was pleased to express his dissatisfaction at the evils brought to light by this report: that manufacturers were in the habit of working large numbers of children in the night, whereby the physical development of persons of those tender years was checked; and that there was reason to fear that in the manufacturing districts the future generation would grow up even weaker and more crippled than the existing one was stated to be.

In obedience to the before-named order, the ministers, charged with the execution of it, instituted an inquiry as to the causes of this degenerate physical state of the manufacturing population, as represented in the report of Lieutenant General von Horn; and it appeared from the unanimous testimony of the provincial authorities who were examined on the subject, that it was to be traced partly to this circumstance, that a large number of children, in the earliest stages of their physical developement, were employed in manufactures, in excessive and long continued labour, frightfully disproportionate to their infantine powers. In Berlin, for example, 1510 young persons of both sexes, from eight to eighteen years of age, were found to be employed in factories from eleven to fourteen hours daily in continuous labour, and the same thing was going on to a still greater extent, comparatively, in the Rhenish Provinces. Such employment precludes, in general, all exercise in the open air, and causes injuries which can be traced to the positions in which they work, either sitting, or standing in a stooping posture, or continually moving some one part of the body. They are almost always employed in highly heated apartments, in which the artificial temperature must often rise to the highest degree that is bearable. The atmosphere of these rooms, besides, is often loaded with particles of the material used in the manufactories, and these positively noxious substances must necessarily be swallowed by the children, to the inevitable injury of their health. This is the case, for example, in pin manufactories and in cotton spinning. In some factories the children are kept in constant employment in the night time. Such an unnatural mode of life is evidently calculated to repress the physical growth, and to sow in the body the seeds of ill-health in their earliest years. It puts a stop, in like proportion, to their intellectual and moral advancement; for it deprives them of all opportunity, capability, and power of mental developement, and of the full advantages of school instruction.

The preceding facts show that urgent necessity for legislative interference, felt by the King, to put a stop to such premature, unnatural, and injurious employment of the young operatives in the factories. The same necessity was felt in other countries, and especially in England, whose legislation in this matter deserves particular consideration; for the Act 3 & 4 W. IV., c. 103., several years ago set effective bounds to that manufacturing cupidity, which shows itself in the abuse of the labour of young people.

It was in the densely peopled manufacturing parts of the Rhenish Provinces, that these striking and lamentable evils were most apparent; and in the last Diet of the Provincial

States held there, the following resolutions, as to the necessity of a protecting law, were embodied in the form of a special petition: —

1. That children who have not completed their ninth year shall not be allowed to work in factories.

2. That children shall not be admitted into factories unless they shall produce proof of having attended school for three years: except local circumstances should render a deviation from this condition necessary; which however must be inquired into, and regulated by the local magistrates.

3. That children shall not be allowed to work in factories more than ten hours a day, at the most.

4. That in the course of these ten working hours the children shall have two hours of intervals of rest, one of which shall be at noon, when they shall have exercise in the open air.

The resolutions 1, 2, and 4. were carried unanimously, the third by a majority of 60 to 9.; this minority wishing to fix the limit of employment at eleven hours daily.

These resolutions, which were strongly supported by the Government Commissary at the Diet, appeared to the Ministers of State to form an appropriate ground-work, in all essential particulars, for the wished-for law; and, accordingly, they were mainly followed in framing the regulations for the employment of the young operatives in factories, which were drawn up by the Minister of the Interior and of Police.

It is true that this petition from the Diet of the Rhenish Provinces was the more immediate origin of this law, so imperatively called for; but it was not in these provinces alone that the necessity of it was felt: it was no less apparent in all the manufacturing districts in the kingdom. As the above resolutions were general, and had no reference to any special circumstances belonging to any particular province, there was no internal ground for confining their operation to the Rhenish Provinces; and the Ministers of State did not therefore hesitate, humbly to recommend to

His Majesty, that the regulations should apply equally to the whole kingdom. There was, moreover, a special reason for this. Had the restrictions been confined to the factories of the Rhenish Provinces, it would have subjected them to an unfair competition. If a certain class of young operatives were to be entirely excluded, and the daily labour of another class were to be fixed at a maximum of ten hours, the factories affected by the law would be obliged to employ a greater number of older hands, and consequently the cost of production of the manufactured article would be increased. If, therefore, the restrictions were not general throughout the kingdom, they would operate very disadvantageously upon the manufactures of the Rhenish Provinces.

In explanation of the several provisions of the regulations, declared by the royal cabinet order of the 6th of April, of last year, to be a general law throughout the monarchy, it is to be observed:—

Reg. I. It has been proved by experience, that no child under nine years of age can be regularly employed in a factory without positive injury to its health. The English statute has, therefore, forbidden any child to be so employed in factories under that age; and the States in the Rhenish Provinces came to an unanimous resolution to the same effect. The Ministers of State thought it advisable to extend the prohibition to mining operations, because it is usual to employ children prematurely in that description of work, to the injury of their health.

Reg. II. The necessity of providing a security for the intellectual and moral development of the young factory operatives, was the ground for this second regulation. And here, also, the recommendations of the States have been followed in the most essential particulars, but modified, in this respect; that a dispensation from the three years previous attendance at school could not be allowed, because it was to be expected that, if that were the case, the exception would become the general rule. But the being able to read the mother tongue with fluency, together with a beginning in writing, are held as an equivalent to the object intended by a three years' school attendance, and it was thought advisable to impose this alternative condition previous to children being allowed to work in factories.

Reg. III. The hours of daily employment, fixed by this regulation, is the same as was proposed by the States. The States speak, it is true, of "children" only ; but the expression is not sufficiently precise for a legal enactment, and has been avoided. They mean, under the term children, young people who have reached their tenth year of age, and who may be considered to be in the earlier stages of physical developement. It was necessary, however, to fix a definite boundary for the restrictions intended by the present law. The English have restricted the labour of young persons up to their eighteenth year; but the Minister of State thought that in Germany the completion of the sixteenth year is the period at which, in general, the physical growth is sufficiently matured to admit of greater bodily exertions. It was determined to fix one uniform amount of labour for all operatives who were to be affected by the law, because any classification of the young operatives in factories according to their ages, and any difference in their hours of work, proportioned to their apparent aptitude, could not be laid down. As such a difference must rest on uncertain and purely individual grounds, great difficulties in carrying out such a principle would occur, and the enforcement of regulations for such a purpose could not be accomplished. It is true, that a difference in this respect is laid down by the English law; but it has been held by some to be incapable of application, and by others as unfounded : so that it has been proposed in parliament to repeal this, and to substitute one uniform period of ten hours' work for all factory operatives under eighteen years of age.

Looking to the interest of the manufacturers, it was deemed advisable, in the cases of accidents mentioned in this regulation, to allow a temporary extension of the period of work, to the amount of one hour, under certain conditions therein mentioned, and which is also the case in the English law.

Reg. IV. This regulation modifies the resolution of the provincial States on this head. It provides for a regular interruption of the hours of work, keeping in view that it is not so much the length of the intervals, as the disadvantages of uninterrupted work that have to be regarded ; and that the young people may at reasonable intervals enjoy the benefit of fresh air. The Minister of State considered this regulation preferable to that suggested by the Provincial States, which extended the intervals of rest to thirty minutes, but left the periods of the day at which they should be given to the discretion of the mill-owner.

Reg. VII. This regulation is intended to facilitate the business of control. The observance of this is so important, that the infraction of it renders the offender liable to a special penalty provided in the following regulation, and which is fixed in conformity with the provisions of the National Code, part II. title 20. § 33. 35. 240.

Reg. VIII. The Minister of State thought it necessary to fix a penalty of not less than one, nor more than five thalers, for each child illegally employed, because in the Rhenish Provinces the police courts take cognisance of offences punishable by penalties not exceeding the above sums; and it does not appear desirable that violations of this law should in the first instance be brought within the jurisdiction of the correctional police courts : but in the case of a second offence, the offender will be punished in these last courts. In the older provinces of the kingdom, the jurisdiction of the police authorities is not under these restrictions.

Reg. IX. The dispensation from regular school attendance being always viewed as an exception, and justifiable only in those cases where circumstances render it necessary, it is intended by this regulation to show that in the manufacturing districts, the abridgement of the hours of school attendance is not to be made the rule in the present law ; on the contrary, the local governments are to have the power to order that when the intellectual training of the children has been deficient, and whenever circumstances will admit of it, the duration of school attendance shall be extended.

Reg. X. Besides the sad evils represented by the States in the Rhenish Provinces, as arising out of the cupidity of manufacturers, there were other things, which have been partly touched upon in this paper, relating to the health and morals of the operatives in the factories, of an injurious nature, but so various in their kind that they could hardly be reached sufficiently by a general law. To these belong the bad construction of the factories, occasioning imperfect ventilation, and the absence of proper discipline among the operatives ; by which, in some factories, children are allowed to indulge in ardent spirits and to smoke tobacco, and, by want of a proper separation of the sexes, they are addicted to premature and illicit intercourse. To correct and guard against such evils and immoralities, according to the particular situations, the Ministers of State humbly submitted to His Majesty, that the Ministers, in whose province it falls, shall have power to make such regulations concerning the health and morals of the people as may appear to them desirable for the accomplishment of the benevolent objects of this law.

The Ministers of State believe that by means of these regulations, the condition of a great part of the younger population will be ameliorated, and that both moral and physical deformities in them will be prevented.

The King, participating in the same views, was graciously pleased to order that the measures, thus proposed by the Ministers of State for regulating the employment of youthful operatives in factories, dated the 9th March, 1839, should have the force of law throughout the whole kingdom.

Berlin, the 14th of April, 1840,

The Minister of the Interior and of Police,

VON ROCHOW.

VII. *Employment of Children in the Factories of Switzerland and Austria.*

The following information respecting Switzerland and Austria is extracted from the valuable report of Mr. Symons in the collection of reports presented to the House of Commons, by the Commissioners for inquiring into the condition of the hand-loom weavers: —

In the Canton of Argovia there are several cotton spinning mills. The hours of work are from six in the morning to eleven in the forenoon, and from twelve to half past seven in the evening. The State does not allow any children to be admitted to work in them under *fourteen* years of age, which is, perhaps, the most rigid law on this subject in force; and the mill-owners are obliged to educate the children they employ. Education is there, as elsewhere in Switzerland, compulsory. Mr. Symons visited the school of the Messieurs Herzog of Aarau, where he found reading, writing, arithmetic, and singing taught, the expense being entirely defrayed by the manufacturers.

The Canton of Zurich ranks first, for the extent of its cotton spinning factories. No children under ten years of age are allowed to work in them, and Mr. Symons states that the clergy look very sharply after the enforcement of the law. The children may work twelve hours a day, but they must go to school at least half a day in the week.

The hours of factory labour in Austria are cruelly long, being frequently, in the factories in the interior, fifteen hours a day, exclusive of meal time, and not unfrequently, seventeen hours. The fate of the unhappy children has excited some animadversion, and the question of shortening the hours of work is occupying the attention of the Government. The law, at present, is more attentive to their minds than it is to their bodies; for no child can be employed in a factory who has not been, and does not produce a certificate of having been, a certain number of sessions at school.

VIII. *Law in the State of Massachusetts relative to the education of Children in Factories.*

In my special report to the Secretary of State, "On the Effects of the Educational Provisions of the Factories Act," dated the 28th of January, and ordered by the House of Commons to be printed on the 20th of February 1839, I noticed the law that had been passed for the education of factory children in this State, which is the principal seat of the cotton manufacture in the United States. Since that time, I have procured some farther information on the subject, through the medium of Mr. Charles Sumner, a distinguished American gentleman who visited England last year. He transmitted at my request, a series of questions to the Hon. Horace Mann of Boston, the Secretary of the Board of Education, which Mr. Mann has been so obliging as to answer, in a letter dated the 12th of March, 1840.

The Acts of the State are as follows : —

I. An Act to provide for the better Instruction of Youth employed in Manufacturing Establishments.

"Be it enacted, by the Senate and House of Representatives in General Court assembled, and by the authority of the same, as follows: SEC. 1. From and after the first day of April in the year eighteen hundred and thirty-seven, no child under the age of fifteen years shall be employed to labour in any manufacturing establishment, unless such child shall have attended some public or private day-school where instruction is given by a teacher, qualified according to the first section of the twenty-third chapter of the Revised Statutes, at least three months of the twelve months next preceding any and every year in which such child shall be so employed. SEC. 2. The owner, agent, or superintendent of any manufacturing establishment, who shall employ any child in such establishment contrary to the provisions of this Act, shall forfeit the sum of fifty dollars for each offence, to be recovered by indictment, to the use of common schools in the towns respectively where said establishment may be situated."

[Approved by the Governor, April 16. 1836.]

II. An Act in addition to an Act to provide for the better Instruction of Youth employed in Manufacturing Establishments.

" Be it enacted, by the Senate and House of Representatives in General Court assembled, and by the authority of the same, as follows :

" No person shall be liable to the penalty provided in the Act passed the sixteenth day of April, in the year one thousand eight hundred and thirty-six, entitled ' An Act to provide for the better Instruction of Youth employed in Manufacturing Establishments,' who shall in each year, before employing any child under the age of fifteen years, as in said Act mentioned, obtain and preserve a certificate, signed by the instructor of the school where such child attended at least three months out of the twelve months preceding, as in said Act is provided, that such child has received the instruction in said Act intended to be secured, the truth of which certificate shall be sworn to by the said instructor before some justice of the peace for the county where such instructor resides, and upon said certificate shall also be certified the fact of such oath or affirmation by such justice."

[Approved by the Governor, April 13, 1838.]

Letter which I have received from Mr. Mann :

To L. HORNER, Esq.

" My dear Sir,   Boston, March 12, 1840.

" It is some months since I received from my friend Charles Sumner, Esq., a letter covering a note from yourself, in reference to the education of children employed in manufacturing establishments in Massachusetts. My apology for delaying an answer is, that I was then in the prosecution of inquiries on the very subject,—that I was then unable to furnish you with the information desired, but hoped soon to be enabled to do it.

" In my last Report to the Board of Education, the subject is adverted to in some of its social aspects ; but as a specific answer to your several questions will be likely to bring out with more exactness the information you desire, I will copy and reply to them in their order.

1. Is the attendance at school daily throughout the year, for such a period of each day as shall be equivalent to three months of the ordinary school hours of children not employed in the factories ? or

2. Is the attendance at school daily for three months ; and if so, how many hours each day ?

Ans. The children must attend school three consecutive months.   There is no law regulating the number of hours which shall constitute a school day ; but usage, almost universal in the state, has established six hours, three A. M. and three P. M., as the length of the school day.   Saturday afternoon is always a half-holiday.   Wednesday afternoon is the same in Boston, and in a very few other places.   In some schools, very small children are not detained the whole time ; but far the most prevalent rule is six hours for a day, and five and a half days for a week.

This rebuts your presumption, viz. " 3. I presume that it does not mean that the children leave the factory for three months in order to attend school daily, during the ordinary hours."

4. How many days in the week must the children attend school, and what is the minimum of time each day ?

This, also, is answered above.

5. When the children are at school, does the work at which they are employed cease in their absence, or are other children employed as their substitutes ?

Ans. Other children are employed.   When there are four children in a family, they can send three to the factory, and one to the school the year round.

6. If substitutes, or a system of relays is acted upon, how is the time divided among the children employed in one factory?

Ans. The facts do not exist on which this question is raised.

7. At what periods of the day do the children attend school?

Ans. Usually from nine to twelve A. M., and from one to four P. M.

8. Are schools kept open at such hours of the morning and evening, as will accommodate them to the factory hours?

Ans. No.

9. Do the children pay for the instruction; if so, how much? If not, how is the schoolmaster paid, and how much for each child?

Ans. The schools are *free.* The law of the State requires every town to maintain schools of certain grades and periods of duration, according to its population. If the schools are not maintained, the town is severely mulcted. To these schools every child has a right to go; at least every child between the ages of four and sixteen, and many go both under and over that age; and so pervading and deep is the feeling of this right, that it is never thought of as a political, but as a natural one by the people. No one defends it, for no one questions it. Any child would be as much surprised if called upon to pay for attending one of our public schools, as he would be if called upon to pay for the succession of the seasons, — for air or sunshine. The provisions of the law, in regard to the amount of schooling, are nugatory; for there is not a town in the State which, with one exception, does not go voluntarily far beyond the requisitions of the law. This exception applies to a class of towns which are obliged to keep a school of a higher class, in addition to the district school. As such a school is generally central, and the benefits of it cannot be enjoyed by residents in the exterior parts of the town, it is generally opposed by them; and in about thirty towns in the State this requisition is not observed. More and more of those towns are, however, every year complying with the law.

10. Is there any inspection of the factories, to ascertain that this law is obeyed?

Ans. None, except the thousand-eyed police of New England, *Public Opinion.*

11. As regards the employment of children under fifteen, at what hour do they commence work in the morning, and leave off in the evening? How many hours in the day are they employed, and what intervals from labour are allowed for meals?

Ans. In winter at seven in the morning, and leave work at seven in the evening. In summer, generally one hour earlier in the morning.

Children, when employed, work the same number of hours as adults; about twelve hours in summer, *exclusive* of meal hours, say half an hour at breakfast, and three quarters of an hour at dinner; in winter, eleven or twelve hours, including the hours for meals : generally the labour of every day is alike. In some establishments, one half of Saturday (the pay-day) no work is required; but as much of the work is job work, there is very little difficulty in securing industry. A holiday at paying off operates unfavourably.

12. Is the labour of every day alike? Do they work on Saturday the same number of hours as the other days?

Ans. Yes, excepting as above.

13. Is there any law to limit the age at which children may be employed? If so, what is the earliest age at which they are admissible?

Ans. There is no law on the subject, but young children are very rarely employed.

14. Can children of any age be employed, and for the same number of hours as adults?

Ans. There is no statute to forbid it, but the *unwritten* law does not allow it.

15. What proof is required of the child's being fifteen, in order to claim exemption from attendance at school?

Ans. The fact of being fifteen must be judicially proved,

if called in question, like any other fact; that is, if a manufacturer were indicted for a violation of the law, the Government must prove the three facts, — employment, — that the child is under fifteen, — that he has not attended the requisite school for three months within the twelve preceding months.

Having answered your questions, I will take the liberty to make a few general statements, not strictly coming within them.

The law is a recent one. Before its passage, many manufacturers had taken measures to educate, to some extent, the children in their employ; but this depended upon the character of the owner, or of a few influential individuals in a corporation. Since the law, many observe it who would not have observed the duty. I think the law is observed with regard to fourteen fifteenths of all the factory children in the State. The children of American parents, almost without exception, are desirous of giving their children even more schooling than three months in a year. At the printing (calico) establishments, glass manufactories, and other works, where the operatives are mostly foreigners, many parents endeavour to evade the law, and vigilance on the part of the employer is necessary. In cotton and woollen factories *children under fifteen are not usually employed*, except in some cases where poor parents need their wages : older persons are preferred. A certificate of a teacher, sworn to before a justice of the peace, that a child has attended the school of the deponent for the requisite time, and within the requisite time, exonerates the employer: if false, the punishment falls elsewhere. Before the law, morning and evening schools had been established in many places, where children could attend a part of the day, and work a part of it. It is found that these schools have increased with the day-schools; for, to furnish suitable aliment at suitable times to a child's natural appetite for knowledge, is like rolling a stone down hill; it needs, at first, a little impulse *in the right direction*, then its speed constantly accelerates;

it bounds and leaps away of itself, and woe to the man that tries to stop it.

In order to understand, at all, the relative condition of this class of children in Great Britain and in the United States, the wages given, and the amount of necessaries and comforts which those wages will command, must be taken into the account. Children, I believe, work as many hours in a day here as there; but with us in, substantially, all cases the food is wholesome, nutritious, and abundant. The houses, in which they live are dry and warm. In ventilation, however, they are seriously deficient. Practically speaking, fresh air, in this whole country, is considered as a sort of nuisance; and, hitherto, our architects have rather prided themselves upon their contrivances to keep out the pertinacious intruder. This is especially true, in regard to public buildings, churches, court-houses, lecture-rooms, school-houses, &c.: its uses are not understood; God is not thanked for it, men do not enjoy it; the beasts and birds only realise the blessing.

The prices paid for female labour in our cotton mills, exclusive of board and washing, vary from $1, 25, to $4 per week. No class of people is more free and independent. The competition for this kind of labour is very great, so that it is not only well paid, but paid for in *money*,— not in ribands and glass beads, and spurious jewellery. Another point of immense importance is the character of the young women employed in our factories. With as few exceptions as ever need to be made, — but which always must be made when speaking of great classes, — there is a remarkable propriety in their manners, an observance of the decorous usages of civilised society in their conduct, and an unspotted virtue in their lives. In the city of Lowell, from eight hundred to a thousand of them are members of a Lyceum, before which popular lectures are delivered once a week, for more than six months of the year. At half past seven o'clock in the evening they strike work; at eight they appear in the Hall. A more interesting sight cannot be found;

persons who live by their hands, emulous of improving their minds.

Factories exist in Maine, New Hampshire, Rhode Island, Connecticut, New York, New Jersey, and Pennsylvania. There is an old law, I believe, in Connecticut, on the subject of educating this class of children, but I fear it is obsolete.

Having already extended my remarks so far, I will add nothing more, except to assure you of the deep interest I feel in your labour, and of my earnest prayer that the efforts now making on this and its kindred subjects, may lead to human amelioration all over the globe.

With great regard, yours, &c. &c.

HORACE MANN.

Mr. Mann transmitted to me at the same time a copy of the Third Annual Report of the Board of Education. It contains a report from himself to the Board, in which there are the following observations on the education of the young persons employed in the factories : —

"Another subject, respecting which I have sought for information from all authentic sources, and to which I have given especial attention in my circuit through the State, is the observance or non-observance of the law 'for the better instruction of youth, employed in manufacturing establishments.' This law was enacted in April, 1836, and was to take effect on the first day of April, 1837. The substance of its provisions, is, that, no owner, agent, or superintendent of any manufacturing establishment, shall employ any child, under the age of fifteen years, to labour in such establishment, unless such child shall have attended some public or private day-school, where instruction is given by a legally qualified teacher, at least three months of the twelve months, next preceding any and every year in which such child shall be so employed. The penalty for each violation is fifty dollars. The law has now been in operation sufficiently long, to make manifest the intentions of those to whom its provisions apply, and whether those humane provisions are likely to be observed or defeated. From the information obtained, I feel fully authorised to say, that, in the great majority of cases, the law is obeyed. But it is my painful duty also to say, that, in some places, it has been uniformly and systematically disregarded. The law is best observed in the largest manufacturing places. In several of the most extensive manufacturing villages and districts, all practicable measures are taken to prevent a single instance of violation. Some establishments have contributed most generously towards the schools; and, in one case (at Waltham), a corporation, besides paying its proportion of taxes for the support of the public schools in the town, has gratuitously erected three schoolhouses, — the last in 1837, a neat, handsome, modern, stone building, two stories in height, — and maintained schools therein, at a charge, in the whole, upon the corporate funds, of a *principal* sum of more than seven thousand dollars. It would be improper for me here to be more particular than to say, that these generous acts have been done by the ' *Boston Manufacturing Company*' ; though all will regret, that the identity of the individual members who have performed these praiseworthy deeds, should be lost in the generality of the corporate name.

" Comparatively speaking, there seems to have been far greater disregard of the law, by private individuals and by small corporations, especially where the premises are rented from year to year, or from term to term, than by the owners or agents of large establishments. Private individuals, renting an establishment for one, or for a few years, — intending to realise from it what profits they can, and then to abandon it and remove from the neighbourhood or town where it is situated, — may be supposed to feel less permanent interest in the condition of the people who are growing up around them, and they are less under the control of public opinion in the vicinity. But, without seeking an explanation of the cause, there cannot be a doubt as to the fact.

" It is obvious, that the consent of two parties is necessary to the infraction of this law, and to the infliction of this highest species of injustice upon the children whom it was designed to protect. Not only must the employer pursue a course of action, by which the godlike powers and capacities of the human soul are wrought into thorough-made products of ignorance, and misery, and vice, with as much certainty and celerity as his raw materials of wool or cotton are wrought into fabrics for the market by his own machinery; but the parent also must be willing to convert the holy relation of parent and child into the unholy one of master and slave, and to sell his child into ransomless bondage for the pittance of money he can earn. Yet, strange to say, there are many parents, not only of our immigrant, but of our native population, so lost to the sacred nature of the relation they sustain towards the children whom they have brought into all the solemn realities of existence, that they go from town to town, seeking opportunities to consign them to unbroken, bodily toil, although it involves the deprivation of all the means of intellectual and moral growth ; — thus pandering to their own vicious appetites, by adopting the most efficient measures to make their offspring as vicious as themselves.

" If, in a portion of the manufacturing districts in the State, a regular and systematic obedience is paid to the law, while, in other places, it is regularly and systematically disregarded, the inevitable consequences to the latter will be obvious, upon a moment's reflection. The neighbourhood or town where the law is broken will soon become the receptacle of the poorest, most vicious, and abandoned parents, who are bringing up their children to be also as poor, vicious, and abandoned as themselves. The whole class of parents, who cannot obtain employment for their children at one place, but are welcomed at another, will circulate through the body politic, until, at last, they will settle down, as permanent residents in the latter ; like the vicious humours of the natural body, which, being thrown off by every healthy part, at last accumulate and settle upon a diseased spot. Every breach of this law, therefore, inflicts direct and positive injustice, not only upon the children employed, but upon all

the industrious and honest communities in which they are
employed; because its effect will be to fill those communities
with paupers and criminals; — or, at least, with a class of
persons, who, without being absolute, technical paupers,
draw their subsistence, in a thousand indirect ways, from the
neighbourhood where they reside; and without being absolute criminals in the eye of the law, still commit a thousand
injurious, predatory acts, more harassing and annoying to
the peace and security of a village than many classes of
positive crimes.

" While water-power only is used for manufacturing purposes, a natural limit is affixed, in every place, to the extension of manufactories. The power being all taken up, in
any place, the further investment of capital and the employment of an increased number of operatives, must cease.
While we restrict ourselves to the propulsion of machinery
by water, therefore, it is impossible that we should have
such an extensive manufacturing district as, for instance,
that of Manchester in England, because we have no streams
of sufficient magnitude for the purpose. But Massachusetts
is already the greatest manufacturing state in the Union.
Her best sites are all taken up, and yet her disposition to
manufacture appears not to be checked. Under such circumstances, it seems not improbable that steam-power will be
resorted to. Indeed, this is already done to some extent.
Should such improvements be made in the use of steam, or
such new markets be opened for the sale of manufactured
products, the capitalists, by selecting sites where the expense
of transportation, both of the raw material and of the
finished article, may be so reduced as, on the whole, to make
it profitable to manufacture by steam, then that agency will
be forthwith employed: and, if steam is employed, there is
no assignable limit to the amount of a manufacturing population that may be gathered into a single manufacturing district. If, therefore, we would not have, in any subsequent
time, a population like that of the immense city of Manchester, where great numbers of the labouring population live in
the filthiest streets, and mostly in houses which are framed

back to back, so that in no case is there any yard behind
them, but all ingress and egress, for all purposes, is between
the front side of the house and the public street, — if we
would not have such a population, we must not only have
preventive laws, but we must see that no cupidity, no con-
tempt of the public welfare for the sake of private gain, is
allowed openly to violate or clandestinely to evade them. It
would, indeed, be most lamentable and self-contradictory,
if, with all our institutions devised and prepared on the hy-
pothesis of common intelligence and virtue, we should rear a
class of children, to be set apart, and, as it were, dedicated to
ignorance and vice.

" After presenting to the Board one further consideration,
I will leave this subject. It is obvious, that children of ten,
twelve, or fourteen years of age, may be steadily worked in
our manufactories without any schooling, and that this cruel
deprivation may be persevered in for six, eight, or ten years,
and yet, during all this period, no very alarming outbreak
shall occur to rouse the public mind from its guilty slumber.
The children are in their years of minority, and they have
no control over their own time or their own actions. The
bell is to them what the water-wheel and the main shaft are
to the machinery which they superintend. The wheel re-
volves, and the machinery must go ; the bell rings, and the
children must assemble. In their hours of work, they are
under the police of the establishment; at other times, they
are under the police of the neighbourhood. Hence this state
of things may continue for years, and the peace of the
neighbourhood remain undisturbed, except, perhaps, by a few
nocturnal or sabbath-day depredations. The ordinary move-
ments of society may go on without any shocks or collisions,
— as, in the human system, a disease may work at the vitals
and gain a fatal ascendancy there, before it manifests itself on
the surface. But the punishment for such an offence will not
be remitted, because its infliction is postponed. The retribution, indeed, is not postponed, it only awaits the full completion of the offence ; for this is a crime of such magnitude,
that it requires years for the criminal to perpetrate it in, and

to finish it off thoroughly in all its parts. But when the children pass from the condition of restraint to that of freedom, — from years of enforced but impatient servitude to that independence for which they have secretly pined, and to which they have looked forward, not merely as the period of emancipation, but of long-delayed indulgence ; — when they become strong in the passions and propensities that grow up spontaneously, but are weak in the moral powers that control them, and blind in the intellect which foresees their tendencies ; — when, according to the course of our political institutions, they go, by one bound, from the political nothingness of a child to the political sovereignty of a man,—then, for that people, who so cruelly neglected and injured them, there will assuredly come a day of retribution. It scarcely needs to be added, on the other hand, that if the wants of the spiritual nature of a child, in the successive stages of its growth are duly supplied, then a regularity in manual employment is converted from a servitude into a useful habit of diligence, and the child grows up in a daily perception of the wonder-working power of industry, and in the daily realisation of the trophies of victorious labour. A majority of the most useful men who have ever lived, were formed under the happy necessity of mingling bodily with mental exertion."

IX. *Recent Proceedings in Russia relative to Children employed in Manufactures.*

(*Received 9th June*, 1840.)

By the kindness of Viscount Palmerston, I have received the following documents from St. Petersburg : —

1. *Copy of a Note from* COUNT NESSELRODE *to the* MARQUESS OF CLANRICARDE, *respecting the Regulations enforced in Russia for the Employment and Education of Children working in Factories.*

" In reply to the note which his Excellency the Marquess

of Clanricarde has been pleased to address to the Ministers
of his Imperial Majesty, dated the 17th of April last, for the
purpose of ascertaining in what manner the labour of children employed in manufactures is regulated in Russia, and
what are, in general, the regulations in force on that subject,
the undersigned has the honour to transmit herewith, in the
French language, a summary of the information relating to
this matter, which has been communicated by the Minister
of Finance. He embraces the opportunity of assuring his
Excellency," &c. &c.

(Signed)   " Nesselrode.

" St. Petersburg, the 25th May, 1840."

2. *Memorandum by the Minister of Finance.*

Manufacturing by machinery not having as yet extended
very greatly in Russia, especially spinning mills, and the
number of children employed in factories being in general
very inconsiderable; a strong necessity has not as yet been
felt, for regulating, by positive laws, either the duration of
the labour of the children, or the circumstances connected
with their employment, and therefore no regulations have
hitherto been promulgated respecting them.

But considering that the number of children, occupied in
that description of labour, is likely to increase every year, as
manufacturing establishments and machinery multiply, the
Imperial Government has deemed it indispensable to take
such preparatory measures as will lead to legislative enactments hereafter.

His Majesty the Emperor having been graciously pleased
to direct his attention also to this important object, issued
orders that means should be devised for watching over the
moral education of the operatives employed in factories; and,
in furtherance of that supreme command, a report was submitted to the Emperor by the Minister of Finance, about the
end of the year 1833; and upon the representations contained
in that report, the Council of Manufactures established at
Moscow were enjoined to require of the manufacturers that
they should not debilitate the children by daily labour pro-

longed beyond just limits, and that they should do every thing in their power to obtain for all the children, and especially for those belonging to the inhabitants of Moscow, an education suitable to their sphere of life; either by the establishment of schools, or courses of instruction in the factories themselves, or by sending the children to other schools. The same department of the Council of Manufactures was likewise directed to see to the enforcement of these measures.

At a later period the Emperor, during his stay at Moscow, about the end of the year 1837, was pleased to issue a farther order, that the necessary steps should be taken to preserve as much as possible the children employed in factories from the contagion of vice, and to procure for them a religious education. For the purpose of accomplishing that salutary object, it is proposed to open in the seventeen parochial schools recently established at Moscow, Sunday schools for these children, where they shall be instructed in religion, and taught to read, to write, and to draw; the two sexes separately; and to make it obligatory upon the manufacturers to see that the children they employ do attend these schools. This plan will be carried into effect as soon as the authorities of the University at Moscow shall order these schools to be opened; and it will be afterwards established in the other towns and governments, as soon as local circumstances shall show that it will be useful.

With regard to the age at which children may be admitted to work in factories, and the amount of their daily labour; both subjects have been under consideration, and will not fail to be duly examined.

APPENDIX (A.).

Notes of a recent Inquiry respecting the Employment of Children in Calico Print Works in Lancashire, by L. HORNER.

The employment of the children is to prepare the smooth surface of colouring matter, on which the carved block is pressed, to take up the colour that is to be transferred to the cloth. There is a circular frame, like the side of a sieve, upon which a fine woollen cloth is stretched, and on this the colour is spread. The pot of colour stands by the side, and a child, who assists the man who prints, transfers the colour from the pot to the sieve, spreads it over the cloth with a flat brush, to make a smooth surface. This is called *tearing*, and the child who performs the operation, whether male or female, is called the *tear-boy*. Every printer has a table and a tear-boy. In some large establishments there are as many as 200 tables; but I am told that they are seldom all at work at one time, from a half to a third being idle. Thus, in an establishment where there are 200 tables, there may be from 100 to 120 children employed; and as in busy times they work all the 24 hours, with a double set of hands, the number of children will be doubled. Thus, the number of children employed in the calico print works of the United Kingdom must be immense. In the immediate neighbourhood of a small town in Lancashire there are nearly 1000 tables.

The work is very irregular; at some seasons they are comparatively idle, while at others they are so busy that they work from an early hour in the morning to late at night; sometimes they work the 24 hours without ceasing, with a double set, each twelve hours; sometimes from six to six, sometimes from twelve to twelve: and this is technically termed *twelving*.

When any printing is going on, the tear-boys must be

there, and they perform their work *standing*. The temperature of the room should not be less than 70°, and the air should be rather humid.

I was informed by Mr. H., surgeon of W., who grants the certificates of age for the children employed in the factories there, that a fortnight ago three children were brought before him wanting certificates of 13 years of age; that he rejected them all, because he was satisfied they were not thirteen; that upon his doing so, the mothers of two of them got very angry, and said that it was very hard they could not get certificates for full time for their children to work in the factory, when they had been working *six years* in the print-works belonging to the same firm, without any interference with them.

When they can get passed for 13 years of age, so as to be able to get the wages of 12 hours' work, they leave the print-works, and come to the factories.

The following statements were made to me by persons who had the best means of knowing the facts with accuracy, and on whose testimony I place every reliance : —

That it is by no means uncommon for children to work as tear-boys as early as *six* and *seven* years of age ; and that when there is a pressure for hands, they are sometimes employed as young as five.

That children of six, seven, and eight years of age, may be seen going to work at 12 o'clock of a winter night, in large numbers, sometimes having to walk a mile or two to the works.

That when they are *twelving*, the first set goes at 12 o'clock in the day, and works till 12 at night; that sometimes they do not send away those who have worked from 12 in the day to 12 at night, but let them sleep a few hours in the works, and then set them on again. That there is no interval for meals in the night set, except breakfast; the children taking something with them ; and even their breakfast is taken at the works. That the custom of taking their meals in the works is very injurious, for they do not wash their hands, and they consequently sometimes swallow deleterious colouring matter.

A. B. stated that, being frequently detained in his counting-house late at night, till twelve or one o'clock, he has often in going home, in the depth of winter, met mothers taking their children to the neighbouring print-works, the children crying.

That the print-works are always most busy in the winter time, preparing for the spring trade; that often for weeks together the gas is never extinguished from sun-set to sun-rise; as one set of workers goes another comes: that when not busy enough to require a double set, they work from early in the morning to late at night: that when short of *tearers*, they sometimes keep on a part of those during the day, who have worked all night.

C. D. operative in the cotton-mill of E. F., examined by me, stated, — That his own girl worked at the print-work of ——; that she began when she was about eleven years old; that he has often gone with her between three and four in the morning; that her regular hour should have been twelve at night, but the man for whom she teared, being himself weakly, did not go sooner; that she had three quarters of a mile to go; that she went sometimes at twelve at noon, and came home between ten and eleven at night, for the same reason, viz. her employer being himself unable to stand the fatigue of working till twelve at night.

G. H. employed as a piecer in the same mill at present, as a learner, because they are slack at the print-works to which he belongs, — being examined, stated, — That he was eleven years old a little before last Christmas; that he has been working as a tear-boy at the same works, since he was "going eight;" that when he was "going ten" he has' gone at five in the morning, and staid till ten at night, in the winter time, and every day for three weeks together; that he had his breakfast brought to him, which he ate in the shop; that he had his dinner also brought sometimes, — that he ate it in the shop; that when they were very busy he did not leave the works from five in the morning till ten at night.

J. K., a piecer in the same mill, a delicate-looking boy, apparently between twelve and thirteen years of age, being examined, stated, — That he had worked better than four years as a tear-boy in the same works; that he often went at twelve o'clock at night for a fortnight together, and came home next day about two o'clock; that he never left the work all the time; that he took with him bread and butter and tea, and that he warmed the tea on the stove, and took it about four in the morning; that breakfast was brought to him at eight o'clock; and that he got nothing more until he returned home at two o'clock; that when not *twelving*, he went at six in the morning, and came home at half-past seven in the evening, and at these times went home both to his breakfast and dinner; that he lived about a quarter of a mile from the works.

L. M., the mother of the boy J. K., being examined, stated, — That she has eight children; that she has been deserted by her husband; that her son James was a little past six when he first went to the print-works; that she has many a time carried him there at twelve o'clock at night, in the winter time, and that he has not come home till two o'clock next day.

N. O., the proprietor of a large cotton-mill, employing above 1000 hands, where I have always found the Factory Act honestly obeyed, told me that they suffer severely from the neighbouring print-works carrying off the children under thirteen years of age, where they employ them at any age, and any number of hours, whereby they get higher wages than they can get for working short time in the factories; that when the Factory Act first came into operation, they discharged all under eleven years of age, and they were immediately employed at the print-works more than twelve hours a day, and frequently all night; that they would gladly employ two sets of children, each working half a day, both for the sake of their work, and for the sake of the children themselves, that they might be more at school, and have more play, but that they cannot get them, as the print-works carry them off.

It appears from the work of Dr. Villermé that, in the print-works of France children are employed as tear-boys (*tireurs* or *brosseurs*) from six to twelve years of age, and that every man employed as a printer has a tear-boy. He reckons that in an establishment employing 1000 hands, the proportions of the workers would be as follow : —

Engravers of wood - - -	67
Printers, men and women - -	333
Tear-boys, children of both sexes - -	333
Labourers, and other workmen - -	267
	1000

APPENDIX (B.).

Employment of Children in Coal Mines.

Evidence of three persons examined by Mr. Tuffnell, one of the Commissioners in the Inquiry which took place in June, 1833, previous to the passing of the present Factory Act.

THOMAS GIBSON and GEORGE BRYAN (Witnesses from the coal-mines, Worsley,) examined. *

Have you worked from a boy in a coal mine? — (*Both*) Yes.

What had you to do then? — Thrutching the basket and drawing. It is done by two little boys: one draws a basket, and the other pushes it behind.

Is that hard labour? — Yes, very hard labour.

For how many hours a day did you work? — Nearly nine hours regularly; sometimes twelve; I have worked above thirteen.

How long did you stop for eating? — We used to go in at six in the morning, and took a bit of bread and cheese in our pocket, and stopped two or three minutes; and some days nothing at all to eat.

How was it that you sometimes had nothing to eat? — We were over-burdened. I had only a mother, and she had nothing to give me.

* The answers were given indiscriminately by either witness, but each was required to corroborate what was said by the other.

Then you were sometimes half-starved ? — Yes, I was.

You said that your labour sometimes continued nine hours without intermission ? — Yes, and more than that with nothing except a sup of cold water.

Was your work in the dark ? — By candle-light.

Were there many children in the same way ? —Yes, about 100 in our mine.

Do they work in the same way now exactly ? — Yes, they do ; they have nothing more than a bit of bread and cheese in their pocket, and sometimes can't eat it all, owing to the dust and damp and badness of the air ; and sometimes it is as hot as an oven; sometimes I have seen it so hot as to melt a candle.

Do they never come out of the mine to eat ? — No ; sometimes they work twelve hours without eating. They eat just as their stomachs will take. I have very often taken my dinner down and brought it up again, not being able to eat it, owing to the badness of the air.

What are the usual wages of a boy of eight? When I started I worked three or four months without getting one farthing, and then I got 4d. a day for many years. They used to get 3d. or 4d. a day.

Were you ever beaten when you were a child? — Yes ; many a score of times ; I shall remember as long as I live one beating I got.

What was it? — Both purs * and kicks and thumps.

Are the children often beaten now ? — Not as ill as they used to be, but still they are much beaten sometimes.

Have you ever seen them beaten severely ? — Sometimes with the fist and puncing.†

Are many girls employed in the pits ? — Yes, a vast of those.

As many girls as boys ? — Yes ; there is more in some pits, but there is no rule to go by.

Do they do the same kind of work as the boys ? —Yes, till they get about fourteen years of age, when they get to the

* A pur is a Lancashire term for a kick.
† Puncing it a Lancashire term for kicking.

wages of half a man, and never get more, and continue at the same work for many years.

Did they ever fight together ? — Yes; many days together, many times in a day, I have seen them fight.

Both boys and girls ?—Both boys and girls; sometimes they are very loving with one another.

Are there many bastards produced in the pits ? — Yes, there are many bastards.

Do the women generally have children before they marry ? — A great many have.

Do you think that half have children before they marry ? — I do not think but what they have; they either have, or are big.

Do they know much of household work ? — Yes; they in general make decent wives; some of them better than those who never go into pits; they know what work is, and take to it better.

Which on the whole make the best wives, pit women or others ? — To tell you the truth, I would as soon have one that has not been in the pit; many of them are crooked with going into the pit.

Are there many crooked women? — If they draw for any length of time they become crooked.

Are many boys made crooked by the work ? — In some mines there are many made crooked; in some mines they have not more than two feet high to work in, and four feet wide; in some a yard high, some six or seven feet.

What is the usual height ? — Only one mine has two feet, where they get the best coal we have; a great many three and four feet.

Do the children generally work in the large veins ? — Just as they are called on; but they are obliged to have only children in the two feet mine.

Are the children often ill ? — In general middling well; they are plagued with sore feet and gatherings. I don't but think that many nights they sleep with a whole skin, and their backs gets cuts and bruises with knocking against the mine, it is so low.

Do they work in the wet ? — Yes ; it is very often wet under foot.

Are the low mines or high mines most wet ? — The three feet mines are mostly wet; the two feet ones too; they are wet under foot at times; it makes no difference, winter or summer. I have worked in places where I could not keep the water from my eyes : it ran down from the roof.

Does it frequently run down from the roof ? — When they open new works; but it is many years before it drains in some mines.

Who pays the children, the master or man ? — The man that they labour for.

Is there much black * damp here ? — Yes, a deal of it ; and the candle won't burn ; and then you run out directly, or you are smothered to death.

Do the colliers live to as old an age as other people ? — Very few.

What are their usual complaints ? — Surfeits in general.

Have they much rheumatism ? — Yes, some ; but that comes to young as well as old.

What is that owing to ? — Working in wet work. When I was fifteen I had the rheumatism with working in wet and being starved.

Is it ever cold ? — In some places it is very hot, and in some places very cold.

Can the children read and write ? — Most of them can. There are Sunday-schools and night-schools, where they go to if they can pay for it.

Are they taught without paying for it ? — In Sunday-schools they are, but not in night-schools. In Sunday-schools they don't teach writing.

Could you work without children ? — No; in some places we could not. In the two or three feet mines the fathers are obliged to send them by being over-burdened.

Which is hardest, collier-work or hand-loom weaving ? — Collier-work is far the hardest.

* Fixed air.

WILLIAM BRADSHAW, aged seventeen, examined at Worsley.

Where do you work? — In Walkden Moor, at a place called New Engine.

What is your work? — Drawing for a man.

Describe it? — We have belts and chains round our bodies, and tubs to them.

So the tub is fastened to you? — We have hooks at the ends of the chains, and so that is fastened to the tub, and we pull it about, bending double in this manner (*bending his head down to the table*).

At what time do you go down into the mine? — Mostly we go down at half past five, or between that and six.

When do you come up? — We are uncertain; sometimes at twelve, sometimes before, sometimes after six; sometimes we have been down fourteen hours.

When do you eat? — We eat mostly about ten or twelve; we have no time.

Do you stop working when you eat?—Yes; we stop about a minute or so, and sometimes we work and eat together; when the baskets are full we have more time.

Do you ever stop longer? — Sometimes we stop three or four hours, when our baskets are full.

Have you ever worked a whole day together without stopping to eat? — Yes, we have; and sometimes we can't eat at all for want of something to drink.

Don't you ever take bottles of drink down?—No; they are sure to break.

Do you never take cans? — No; there is no conveniences at all to take any thing about; and if they took cans full, they would be drunk by others.

What do you eat for dinner? — Sometimes bread and cheese, and sometimes bread and butter, and sometimes pies of potatoes and flesh; and in fruit time we get fruit pies.

How often do you have flesh pies? — Sometimes we are a month or two without them; I cannot do with them at all, as they come up again from the mouth.

What makes them come up again? — It is bending in this manner.

You mean that you are sick? — Yes.

Are the boys often sick? — Yes, very often.

Do you breakfast in the mine? — No; my breakfast is coffee and butter-cakes at home, and at night we get potatoes and bacon.

How much do you get a week? — The highest I ever got in my life was 6s. a week, but now about 19s. the last month.

Is that the general wages now? — Yes.

Do girls get the same? — About the same.

Do you work generally bent? — Yes, regularly bent; we never stand up.

Are you often ill? — No; I never was plagued with bad health, not so very much.

How old were you when you went into the mine? — Going nine years since.*

At what age do they usually go into the mine? — There is some that is under six years of age.

Do these little children do the same work as you? — When the little ones can't manage himself the others help; there is two to a basket when one cannot manage it. The little ones bend down just as we do; they hooks the chains to the staples in the baskets, and draw them along; when they thrutch they push with their breasts.

Had you pains in your breast with thrutching? — Yes, sometimes.

Do the girls thrutch? — Yes, when they are little, and when they grow bigger they draw by themselves.

Do the boys and girls work exactly in the same way? — Yes, both exactly in the same way.

Do they ever get crooked with bending? — Yes; there is some as grows crooked as goes in pits, and some as does not.

How are they crooked? — Some in their backs and some in their legs; but very few boys crooked any way; when they grow into men, about thirty or forty years of age, then they starten a growing crooked.

* He was consequently eight when he began to work.

Have the children in pits as good health as those out of pits? — Yes; some is fully better.

Are the people who work out of pits ever crooked? — No; it is not the same as when they are regularly bent in this manner.

What is the weight of the basket you draw? — About four hundred weight.

Have sometimes two little children under six such a basket to draw between them? — Yes; in an easy place, where it is near where he teams the coals, one will do it; some of them have 200 yards to draw the baskets, and when their legs martches they stop and stand in this manner with their hands on the basket as well as they can.

When you go down for a day's work, do you never come up till it is finished? — No, never.

Have you ever worked a week together twelve hours daily? — Yes, in winter; many a time we never see day-light not for three or four days together; we go at dark, and leave at dark.

Did you ever see the children beaten? — Yes, many a time myself; that's very often; both me beat by others, and me beat them; the man what we draw for, if we don't do the way to please him, will very soon give us a beating with the pick-arm*; some will strike with all their might sometimes.

Do they ever break a bone? — No; they mostly hit them over the back, if they can get a convenience.

Have you seen the girls beat? — Yes; they are beat the same as us.

Can the children generally read and write? — Yes.

Can you read? — Yes; and write too a little, just so as to please myself.

Do you know arithmetic? — Not much of that.

Can most read and write as well as you? — Yes; there is as can read and write very well; they learn at night-schools when they come home from the pits in the evening.

How many brothers and sisters have you? — Four brothers

* Handle of the pickaxe.

and one sister alive; one sister died. All my brothers work in a pit.

Did you ever see the fire-damp? — Yes, once; and I have been in it, but I never felt the smart of it, and never saw any body burned by it.

Have you ever seen children brought out of the pit smothered? — Yes, often; myself has been that way.

How did you feel? — It is the same as if I was asleep, and couldn't wake.

How long have you been in recovering? — As soon as ever air can get to us. They fall down groaning; and every thing, strength and all, goes directly. You would think they were dying.

Did you ever see any smothered to death? — No; but they have been sometimes; but it is very few of those accidents happen in this ground.

Are there ever any other sort of accidents? — Yes; some gets their legs broken, some their arms, the roof falling on them.

Have you seen many accidents of this sort?—No; but there has been many accidents of this sort at the same pit where I work.

How many work at your pit? — About thirty-two men, and as many boys and girls.

Do lads ever come to a coal-pit that have been to other work? — Yes; but they sometimes want sadly to go back.

Is the place where you work wet? — It has been wet, but it is dry now.

Is the greater part of the mine dry? — I don't know any place that is dry, except where I work.

How high is it where you work? — It is about three quarters of a yard, and some is about thirty inches or so.

Do you work barefoot? — Some with clogs and some barefoot, boys and girls the same; they take all their clothes off except breeches; girls wear breeches.

How do the girls go down? — Just the same as the boys, by ladders or baskets.

Do they often have rheumatism? — Yes; when they get to thirty or forty.

Is the work constant? — No; we have very little work in summer, but in winter we have plenty; but we get very little for it.

Note by Mr. Tuffnell.

After the examination of the three preceding witnesses, I descended into one of the mines. The mode of entrance was by means of a bucket, in which I was let down to a depth of seventy yards, when we came to a canal, which runs for a considerable distance in a subterranean channel, and drains most of the mines in this district. On this canal I got into a barge which had been prepared to receive me, and which was then made to advance by the boatmen pushing against small staples fastened into the roof, placed there for this purpose. In this way I travelled more than half a mile. The first mine we arrived at was approached by a small tunnel running out laterally from the canal, and in which it was impossible to stand upright, the height not exceeding three or four feet. The place where the working was going on was nothing more than a continuation of this tunnel; the mine was dry throughout, and the temperature slightly below that of the external air. Having returned to the barge, I was landed about half a mile further on at another mine, which was described to me as the best and largest in the district. The approach to it was rather higher than the other, and led to an excavation about eighteen feet square, where the mining process was carried on. This hole was said to be seven feet high, but there were only a few square feet in the centre in which I could stand upright; and as the coal was extracted from the sides, it was obviously impossible for the miners to work in any other position than in one constantly bent. This mine was very damp, and great part of it wet under foot; the roof in many places was dripping, which was also the case throughout a great portion of the canal during my passage along it. As this was said to be the best mine in the place, I cannot much err in coming to the conclusion, both from what I saw, and the evidence of the witnesses given on oath above, that it must appear to every impartial judge of the two occupations, that the hardest labour in the worst room in the worst-conducted factory is less hard, less cruel, and less demoralising than the labour in the best of coal-mines.

THE END.

LONDON:
Printed by A. SPOTTISWOODE,
New-Street Square.

Scholars and Ancestors China under the Sung Dynasty

MARTIN BALLARD

Editorial consultant

PETER MATHIAS

Chichele Professor of Economic History
at Oxford and Fellow of All Souls College

Maps by

STUART JORDAN

METHUEN EDUCATIONAL LTD
LONDON · TORONTO · SYDNEY · WELLINGTON

First published 1973
by Methuen Educational Ltd
11 New Fetter Lane, London EC4P 4EE
© 1973 by Martin Ballard

Filmset and printed Offset Litho by
Cox & Wyman Ltd, Fakenham, Norfolk

SBN 423 88560 X

The Sung painting on the cover is reproduced by courtesy of the Museum of Fine
Arts, Boston.

Contents

Acknowledgments

Permission to reproduce illustrations is gratefully acknowledged as follows:

Radio Times Hulton Picture Library, pages 6, 13, 15.
Camera Press, pages 10 and 52.
By Courtesy of the Trustees of the British Museum, pages 14, 20, 23, 25, 29 (left), 37, 44 (bottom), 59 (bottom), 65.
The Ashmolean, pages 22, 57, 59 (top).
Victoria and Albert Museum, pages (right), 43, 45.
Freer Gallery of Art, Smithsonian Institute, pages 32 and 54.
Haags Gemeentemuseum, page 39.
Collection of the National Palace Museum, Taipei, Taiwan, Republic of China, pages 27, 35, 41, 44 (top), 47.
Rijksmuseum, Amsterdam, page 18.
Museum of Fine Arts, Boston, Massachusetts, page 55.
City Art Gallery, Bristol, page 57.
N. J. Steemson, pages 68, 71, 73.

1 · The Central Nation

The people of China have long known their country as *Chung-hua*, the Central Nation; they recognized that other nations, with other customs, did exist, but existed around the edges of the civilized world. Chinese customs and the Chinese way of life provided the model of excellence. All other people had to be judged by the way in which they measured up to this standard. When the Chinese first came into contact with the peoples of other lands – India, Africa, Europe, Central Asia, the Pacific Islands – they looked upon them alike with a mixture of astonishment and disdain. Their skins were either too light or too dark. They spoke strange, unintelligible languages, had no vision of beauty or respect for ancestors, and they behaved in ways quite shocking to well-brought-up people. All foreigners were barbarians. Only the Chinese were truly civilized; the perfect creation.

In the same way, people in the West talk of the 'Middle East' and the 'Far East', as if all distance were properly measured from their own homes. White men have also long assumed that the colour of their own skins was that chosen by God as the best.

In the year 1126, when our era begins, the Chinese could have made out a strong case to support their good opinion of themselves. They could boast a civilization older than any other. The peoples of Europe were divided into small, warring states; the Norman Conquest of England was still an event within living memory, and the king of France ruled only a small area around Paris. But China was already a unified empire with a population of some 60,000,000. The skills of the artist and the scholar were more highly developed than in any other country.

There had been periods when the territory ruled by the emperors of China had stretched even further. At one time the two massive empires of Rome and China met in the steppe country of Central Asia, and later the T'ang dynasty had controlled the caravan routes across the country which today is Russia. The Sung emperors, who ruled during the period which we shall study, were never noted for their military prowess, nor did they set much store by conquest. Yet their empire at its widest point stretched for over 2,000 miles.

Any country as large as China is likely to have a wide variation in land and climate. In the tropical south, the weather is warm and damp. In the north-

4

CHINA. THE LAND

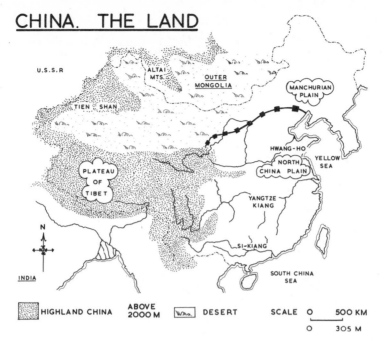

U.S.S.R

ALTAI MTS.

OUTER MONGOLIA

MANCHURIAN PLAIN

TIEN SHAN

HWANG-HO

YELLOW SEA

NORTH CHINA PLAIN

PLATEAU OF TIBET

YANGTZE KIANG

N

SI-KIANG

INDIA

SOUTH CHINA SEA

[_____] HIGHLAND CHINA   ABOVE 2000 M   [~~~] DESERT   SCALE 0 ___ 500 KM
                                                                 0 ___ 305 M

CHINA.   THE CLIMATE

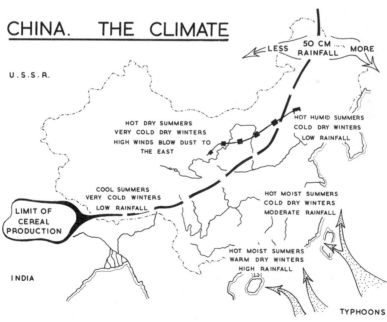

LESS ◄═══ 50 CM RAINFALL ═══► MORE

U.S.S.R.

HOT DRY SUMMERS
VERY COLD DRY WINTERS
HIGH WINDS BLOW DUST TO
THE EAST

HOT HUMID SUMMERS
COLD DRY WINTERS
LOW RAINFALL

COOL SUMMERS
VERY COLD WINTERS
LOW RAINFALL

HOT MOIST SUMMERS
COLD DRY WINTERS
MODERATE RAINFALL

LIMIT OF
CEREAL
PRODUCTION

HOT MOIST SUMMERS
WARM DRY WINTERS
HIGH RAINFALL

INDIA

TYPHOONS

east, the people are exposed to extremes of temperature, and the nights in particular can be very cold. Near the coast the climate is damp, but beyond the mountain barriers of the interior the rainfall diminishes and strong winds carry clouds of dust from the deserts. In the east there are wide plains which in places drop well below sea level. Further west the ground rises steeply until it ends in massive mountain ranges, the peaks of which tower 20,000 feet above sea level. The high land runs from west to east, like the fingers of a hand, and between the fingers flow great rivers carrying the water, which has fallen on the earth's highest mountains, out towards the Pacific Ocean. The civilization of China has always flourished in these river valleys.

The Huang Ho shares with the Nile, the Euphrates and the Indus the distinction of being the cradle of earliest civilization. In its higher reaches it

A trading boat on the upper reaches of the Yangtze Kiang

flows rapidly, eroding the soil and washing it downwards in a brown torrent. When the river begins to flow more gently across the North China Plain, it deposits huge quantities of silt, filling up its own bed. Within historical times it has, therefore, several times changed its course. Over many generations men have tried to keep the river within its banks by building high dykes. The size of this task can be gauged by the fact that after many centuries of silting, the river bed is often higher than the farm land on either side. The whole weight of water has thus to be contained by man-made walls. Any unusually heavy rainfall in the mountains to the west spells danger to the people of the valley.

6

Highland China

When the Huang breaches its dykes, the water pours out over the plains, washing away crops and leaving a deposit of silt which makes the land unusable for many years. Flooding therefore brings famine, and because of this the Huang Ho has long been called 'China's Sorrow'.

By the time of our era there had been a movement both of population and of wealth towards the second great valley, of the Yangtze Kiang, further south. The sources of the two rivers are within a hundred miles of one another, but, while the Huang Ho turns north, the Yangtze flows south through the mountains on the first stage of its 3,200-mile journey to the sea. On the way it is joined by large tributaries which drain water from a wide area, so that, by the time it reaches the China Plain, it carries a volume of water twice that of the Huang Ho. As the Yangtze runs on to the plains, it forms a network of leakes, which store some of the water and so reduce the danger of flood. Despite these natural reservoirs, the water can rise and fall as much as fifty feet between the dykes. The river finally flows into the sea at Shanghai, where it deposits so much silt that the area of land increases by a mile every seventy years.

Further south lies the third valley, of the Si Kiang, which flows into the sea at Canton. Compared with the two great northern rivers the Si is modest in length and in volume of water. Yet it is important in providing another and warmer valley in which civilized life has been able to develop.

The map on page 9 shows how the population of China today is still concentrated along the river valleys, Although China is a vast country, much of her land will support only the sparsest population. To understand the full range of the country's life during this era, we shall look at three contrasts—between lowland and highland, between north and south and between farmers and herdsmen.

Lowland : highland. The majority of people lived on the China Plain to the east. These were the rice farmers, whose way of life has been taken as typically 'Chinese' (see Chapter 6). In the highlands to the west, however, many people lived a completely different kind of existence. A combination of drought and poor soil made farming difficult. After only a few years of cultivation, farm land would be exhausted, and the people had to move to new fields so that the soil could regain its goodness. Naturally, when this shifting cultivation is practised, the land will not support much life. The highland peoples have always been in some measure cut off from the main stream of Chinese life, and even today they tend to look on the lowland folk as strangers, almost foreigners.

8

North : south. Within the lowland zone there is a further distinction between the people of the north and those of the south. According to Chinese tradition, those from the north were under the influence of the element *earth*. This is reflected in their virtues and limitations: they were solid and reliable; but somewhat slow-witted. Those from the south were supposed to be influenced by the element *water*. Their virtues were that they were lively

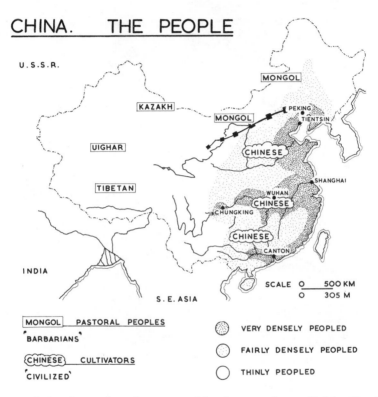

CHINA.   THE   PEOPLE

and clever; their vices, that they were frivolous and unreliable. During our era the south was in the ascendant, so that the vices and virtues of later Sung China were those of the element water.

Farmers : herdsmen. The most important division lies between those who gain their living by farming, of whatever kind, and those who live by tending cattle. Before the introduction of modern agricultural methods, no land could be efficiently farmed unless it was watered by some twenty inches of rain every year. The Tsinling Mountains form a barrier across the north of China beyond which rainfall is sparse. Here man could only live by moving

9

his herds across the dry grassland in search of suitable grazing. Chinese emperors of the 8th Century AD marked the line between the grazing and the farming communities by erecting the Great Wall of China. This is the most fundamental division in the history of man. Only when agriculture is possible can settled communities – cities, towns and villages – develop.

The Great Wall of China

Without settled communities there can be no civilization. Agrarian man has everywhere looked on nomadic man as a barbarian; nomadic man has everywhere looked on agrarian man as soft. It is the same division that existed in Biblical times between the people of Canaan and the desert nomads, or, nearer our own times, between the settled east and the Wild West of America. The Great Wall marked the boundary between civilization and barbarism: to the south lay a great civilization; to the north were barbarian tribes which constituted a continual threat to that civilization.

10

The rulers of China would have been well pleased had the Great Wall succeeded in keeping farmers and herdsmen forever apart. But the problem was too complex to be solved in so simple a manner. As we shall see (page 67) the two groups depended in large measure on one another. At times, when the population on the grassland grew, their needs became greater than their reserves of money and trading goods. It was then very tempting for an ambitious chief to lead his followers across the border. Sometimes these raids assumed the proportions of major invasions.

Our era begins in the year 1125 when the barbarian Chin people invaded the plains of China to drive the Sung dynasty from their first capital of Kaifeng. It ends in the year 1271, when the still more terrible Moguls captured the southern Sung capital of Hanchow.

2 · North Sung and South Sung

Chinese historians have always divided the story of their nation, not into centuries, but into *dynasties*: that is, those periods during which the country was ruled by members of a particular family. The most important of these dynasties have been:

> Chou 1122–771 BC
> Han 206 BC–AD 221
> T'ang AD 618–907
> Sung AD 960–1279
> Ming AD 1368–1662
> Ch'ing AD 1662–1912

Between these were periods of chaos and short-lived or even one-man dynasties.

It can be noted from the table that, once a dynasty had established itself, it had an expectation of life of around 300 years. Traditional Chinese historians emphasized that each dynasty tended to follow the same pattern. It was started by a strong man, who was later built up to be something more than an ordinary human being. This first ancestor gave the dynasty its strength and stability, but gradually problems began to accumulate for his successors.

 a *Invasion from the north*. The threat from the northern herdsmen was never far removed. The later rulers in any dynasty, generally indifferent soldiers, were often reduced to buying off their enemies.
 b *Financial trouble*. Almost inevitably the rulers began to find themselves short of money. This could be for many reasons: payments to barbarians, poor yield from taxes as a result of famine or declining trade, and corruption in the administrative system.
 c *Rebellions*. When the government found itself short of money, it began to neglect the essential work of building dykes and irrigation channels and of relieving famine. Discontent would then begin to boil up in different parts of the country, and in extreme cases it could reach the proportions of large-scale rebellion.

Perhaps most serious of all, the later rulers of a dynasty were men of very different mettle from its founder. While he had come to the top by the force of his personality, they were born and bred in the soft atmosphere of the court.

By the beginning of our era the Sung dynasty had faithfully followed this pattern. The family fortunes had been founded in the 10th Century by the Emperor T'ai Tsu (*Excellent Ancestor*). As befitted the founder of one of the great ruling houses of China, he was a man of great gifts. As well as being an able soldier, who succeeded in bringing peace after years of bloodshed, he was a scholar of repute. His successors had maintained a high tradition of scholarship but completely failed to balance it with military virtues. The dynasty's record on the northern frontier had not been impressive. The barbarian kingdoms of Liao and Hsi-Hsia had conquered land far south of the Great Wall, and demanded heavy tribute in money and silk every year. Within China also discontent was widespread. Small risings were common, and then, early in the 12th Century, the south erupted in a major rebellion, in which over four million were said to have lost their lives. The historians recorded a speech, supposedly made by the rebel leader, in which he registered the discontent of his followers.

 The nation should operate on the same principle as that of a family. What kind of a family would it be if the sons worked hard all year round,

12

to till and to weave, yet received little to eat and little to wear, while their father took away all the fruits of their labour and wasted them, brutally lashed them according to his whims, and often lashed them to death without showing any mercy? If you were one of the sons, could you stand continuously such wanton brutality? The government exacts from us

*Portrait of T'ai Tsu,
founder of the Sung dynasty*

everything it can and presents it to the northern barbarians. The wasteful luxuries the government enjoys and the annual tribute it pays to the enemies are made of the blood of the Southern Chinese. Though we work hard all year round, we have never had a full stomach, and our wives and children suffer constantly from cold and hunger.

The Sungs were ill equipped to meet such a combination of threats from outside and from within their own territories, for in military terms theirs was probably the weakest of all the major dynasties. For this they had to thank T'ai Tsu, the excellent ancestor himself. He was never able to forget that he had started as a soldier and won the imperial title by force of arms. What was possible to him was equally possible to others. He therefore took the drastic step of depriving his generals of all real power.

13

This was to have a profound effect on the dynasty which he founded. It was true that none of his successors would ever be threatened by an over-mighty general. Even in time of war – even when a city was under siege – the generals were made subordinate to civilian officials, who were totally ignorant of the art of warfare. As a result no ambitious man would ever join the army. The profession of soldiering had never had a high status in China. An old proverb declared that 'good men should never become soldiers as good iron

Kuan-ti, God of War
(17th–18th Century)

should not be used to make nails'. In Sung China the position of the soldier reached an all-time low. Vast sums of money were spent on keeping an enormous army on the northern frontier, but both officers and men were of the poorest quality and very often neglected by the government. A contemporary poem describes the feelings of these dispirited and forgotten men.

> Out here on the frontier, the autumn wind is wicked
> And all us soldiers haven't got enough upon our backs.
> That clothing-issue orderly – will he come or won't he?
> With nights as cold as armour, it's hard to sleep a wink.
> But back home at the capital the clever gents are snug enough.

It is perhaps to the credit of Chinese civilization that skill in warfare cannot be numbered among its achievements. In fifteen hundred years there had been no real advance in military technique. Unlike the horsemen who harried them along the frontier, the Chinese never became proficient in methods of attack. When under pressure, their generals shut themselves up behind city walls, and tried to wear down the patience of the opposition. Chinese military history is a record of long sieges and sometimes of dreadful massacres. Military engineers were skilled in constructing fortifications, and also in making elaborate machines for attacking walled cities. 'Stand-up' battles, however, which are so much a part of Western history, were rare.

This reliance on defence meant that the initiative always lay with the enemy. While the Chinese army was cumbersome and inefficient, the horsemen from the north were swift and mobile. Confronted by such an irritating

A Chinese war chariot

opponent, the imperial generals were always prepared to fall back on trickery and intrigue. Promises and threats were recognized weapons of war; espionage and disguise were developed to a fine art. As a last resort, if the enemy could not be defeated, he could always be bribed.

The Sung Empire, therefore, developed serious weaknesses. In the face of rebellion and invasion from the north, emperors found themselves becoming increasingly short of money with which to pay the huge, inefficient army. The dynastic pattern was repeating itself once again, and nowhere was this more evident than in the imperial court itself. The Emperor Hui Tsung, who ruled at the imperial capital of Kaifeng at the beginning of our era, had many virtues, but they were hardly suited to the needs of the moment. It was said of him that he 'would have been a very great man indeed, if he had not unfortunately been a king'. Hui Tsung was a man of the highest culture, endowed with a passionate love of flowers and of beautiful women. Few could excel him as an artist and a poet. Some of his sensitive and beautiful paintings have survived as a testimony to this side of his personality (see page 55).

For many years China's most troublesome neighbour had been the barbarian state of Liao. Hui Tsung was therefore delighted when he heard that a rebellion had broken out in the northern part of that country. It seemed an ideal opportunity for the Chinese to win back some territory which the Liao kings had captured from them. An arrangement was therefore made with the rebels. The Chinese armies would invade Liao from the south, while their new allies came down to meet them from the north. Half of the plan worked very well: the rebels, who called themselves Chin (*Golden*), routed the armies of Liao in the north. But the Chinese armies in the south were much less successful. At the end of the war Hui Tsung therefore found that he had won back much less than he had expected. He protested to his allies, but unfortunately his army's poor showing had only served to give further courage to the Chin conquerors. Instead of giving him more land, in 1125 they rode on even further south, into the North China Plain.

As Chinese resistance crumbled, the Emperor abdicated his throne, for it seemed clear that Heaven had deserted him. In 1126 Kaifeng fell. Both Hui

THE SOUTHERN SUNG DYNASTY

Tsung and the newly appointed emperor, with their entire household of 3,000 people, were taken north into captivity, dressed in the blue robes customarily worn by servants.

Despite this terrible defeat, Chinese resistance was not yet broken. Further south a Sung prince, called K'ang, gathered the remains of the imperial army, and in 1130 the Chin advance was halted on the Yangtze River by a battle at the Huangt'ien Tang ford. K'ang was able to establish himself as emperor, under the title, Kao Tsung (*High Ancestor*). But, before he could be left in

16

peace in his new capital, Hanchow, he had to agree to call the Chin ruler his 'younger uncle' and pay him a yearly tribute in silver and silk.

The Chin rulers set up their capital in the city which is now Peking, and slowly China began to overcome its conquerors with weapons more subtle than any used in battle. As the herdsmen settled down to live among the Chinese, they began to learn Chinese ways. The ancient civilization had survived, despite its military weakness, because it could take invaders and absorb them into itself. Before long there were two Chinese states: Chin in the north and Sung in the south. Even before the fall of Kaifeng, the south had been growing in wealth and importance. Southern Sung was, by Chinese standards, small, and, by any standards, militarily weak. But during the century-and-a-half which passed before new invaders appeared from the north, China reached a peak of civilization which had scarcely been surpassed, even in the greatest days of Han or T'ang, and which was far in advance of any other civilization to be found on earth at that time.

3 · Order and duty

The invaders from the north could be said to have become Chinese when they came to accept certain ideas which lay at the root of all Chinese patterns of thought. In the West we are inclined to look on people first of all as *individuals*. We therefore have a lot to say about our rights and jealously defend individual freedom of thought and of action. The Chinese, on the other hand, have always looked on people first of all as *members of the community*. It follows that they should be more concerned about men's duties than about their rights.

These assumptions, on which society was founded, were first put into ordered form by the philosopher Kung Fu Tsu (better known by his westernized name Confucius). He was not interested in deep religious questions about such issues as life after death. The responsibility of every man and woman was to master the life which faced him here on earth, not to indulge in high-flown questioning. Kung Fu Tsu hated all kinds of disorder. Every

Lid of a
round box

person, he declared, had his appointed place in the order of things. Virtue lay in fulfilling faithfully the duties of his position. Chaos threatened when men neglected the ancient customs and started following their own inclinations. Confucianists therefore always laid great stress on the past. Members of each generation had to preserve the order of society by following the good examples of their ancestors.

Every individual was born with responsibilities to fulfil. These were centred around the fundamental human relationships – between parent and child, husband and wife, older brother and younger brother, master and servant, ruler and ruled. In each case there was a two-way responsibility: the inferior owed respect and service to the superior, but the superior could not use his position for his own selfish advantage. In the ordered society which Kung Fu Tsu yearned after, people would be able to depend on one another because everyone, high and low, was fulfilling his or her duty in a spirit of contentment.

Parent : child. The most basic human relationship was that which bound the generations within the unit of the family. The whole Chinese structure of good and evil rested on the duty which a child owed to the parent who gave him life and cared for him. This duty did not end when the child grew up and reached maturity, and the Chinese have always been deeply shocked at the way that Westerners are prepared to abandon their parents to an old age of poverty and loneliness. A failure in respect for parents was treated as the most serious possible crime. Indeed the traditional code of law laid down that the punishment for striking a parent should be death. Even if such a sentence was rarely carried out, the law was an expression of the horror felt at such an unnatural act. The respect shown by the child for the parent was more than an expression of gratitude and love; it was symbolic of his awareness of his duty within society, of his debt to his ancestors and to those set over him within the state.

The Chinese father had considerable authority over his children, but parenthood also involved responsibilities as well as power. The brutal or the negligent father was thought to have forfeited the right to the respect of his children. Chinese children were rarely beaten and were spoken to courteously by adults. All excesses of emotion – whether of love or anger – were frowned upon, but parents took pleasure in giving their children presents of toys or sweets. Boys in particular were brought up to a completely different code of conduct from boys in the West. From earliest childhood the European boy was expected to develop the instincts of a warrior. To this end he was encouraged to be aggressive and to join in dangerous sports. The Chinese boy, on the other hand, like his sister, was encouraged to be obedient, good natured and gentle. He was told stories, not about brave warriors, but about dutiful sons who went to the greatest lengths to care for their parents in adversity. The heroes that a society provides for its young may be said to

Chinese artists – more than the artists of any other country – enjoyed painting children. These children are playing with hobby horses. (Ming)

reflect the values of that society. To the Chinese, obedience and duty, reflected in the fundamental relationship between one generation and the next, provided the basic framework for life.

Husband : wife. In the same way, the relationship between a husband and wife had to be founded on mutual respect. The fact that the husband was considered superior to his wife in no way justified him in neglecting or mal-treating her. His concern and care for her was properly matched by her obedience and respect for him.

Arrangements for a marriage were usually concluded when the parties were still only six or seven years old. Negotiations were generally conducted through matchmakers, who were respected members of the community. A boy's parents aimed to provide their son with a hard-working, even-tempered bride, who would be physically capable of bearing him children. The arrangement would be sealed by an exchange of gifts. In the course of time the girl would move to live in her husband's house. The first years of her stay there must have been very hard. The homesick child had to do the most

20

menial of jobs and learn at all times to treat her husband and his parents with proper respect. If she sat at the family table at all she occupied the lowest seat.

In many country areas it was the custom that one year after the marriage the mother-in-law would give the girl a sheet of good silkworm eggs. She was then charged with hatching them and tending the silk. If she carried out this task satisfactorily she won the favour of her mother-in-law, and her position in the family improved. The great event in her life was the birth of her first child. From the moment that she became pregnant her husband started to treat her in a distant and casual manner, lest, by showing her affection, he might tempt fate too far. By presenting her husband with a child the young wife fulfilled her highest duty. From that time onwards her place in the home was well established.

Elder brother : younger brother. The same pattern was extended to relationships between brothers and sisters. The younger always had to give proper respect to the elder. The law therefore laid down that a boy who struck his elder brother should be liable to a sentence of two-and-a-half-years' forced labour, while the boy who struck his elder cousin could receive a hundred strokes of the rod.

The same rules applied in everyday dealings between friends. The younger man was expected to give proper deference to the elder. In this way the follower of Confucius could show himself to be *chung-tze*, a true gentleman.

Master : servant. All Confucian relationships lay between one person who was the higher and another who was the lower. The most clear-cut example of this was that between master and servant. Since the master was in every way the superior of his servant, he could expect obedience and respect without question. Yet the master had his responsibilities as well as his privileges. Though he had the right to enjoy the fruits of his servant's work, he could not exploit him or withhold his proper reward. Unhappily practice did not always match up to theory, but, as long as times were good and food was available for all, the Chinese servants, and employed men generally, appear to have been reasonably happy with their lot.

Ruler : ruled. The ties which united the emperor with his subjects were essentially the same, only on a larger scale, as those which tied a father to his son. The subject owed his ruler absolute obedience and absolute respect. Indeed, since the emperor was more than human, he could expect the worship of his people.

But even this was no one-sided relationship, for the emperor was responsible for providing his country with the security in which people could live a good life. Confucians believed that a good society could only exist in an atmosphere of peace and prosperity. In the words of a philosopher:

> If beans and millet were as plentiful as fire and water, such a thing as a bad man would not exist among the people.

It was therefore quite wrong for a ruler to expend his country's resources in wars aimed at extending his own power. In almost all other societies rulers have been judged largely on their success in warfare, but in 2,000 years not a single Chinese writer ever gloried in bloodshed.

A servant (18th Century)

The people therefore properly looked to the emperor for peace and security. It may seem more surprising that they also looked to him for freedom from natural disasters such as drought and flood. It was not enough for him to maintain irrigation channels and dykes in good order; he had also to 'keep favour with Heaven' so that calamities should be averted. The most solemn occasion in the Chinese year therefore was when the emperor went to the shrines to pray to Heaven on behalf of his people. All the sacred actions were rehearsed for days before the festival so that everything should be done properly. Every action in the splendid pageantry had its hidden meaning. If the elements were kind and the harvests good, men would know that Heaven

22

accepted the sacrifice. But if disaster came to the land, then people would begin to wonder whether perhaps the emperor had lost favour. At such times there was likely to be unrest and rebellion in different parts of the country, for the people no longer felt secure in the protection of their emperor. The order of the universe was out of joint and everything that ought to be tidy and stable was therefore thrown into chaos.

The idea that human society was all of a piece with the universe found expression in the rites of ancestor worship. The family unit did not consist only of its living members. The living were bound to the dead in a 'continuity of incense and fire'. Five times a year the family gathered – from the oldest to the youngest members – to make sacrifices to those from past generations who had given them life. A special meal was prepared and paper money was burnt as a symbol of the fact that the living were still prepared to tend the needs of the

The Confucian deity T'ien Kuan
Lord of Heaven (Ming)

An 'immortal' ancestor
(Ming)

dead. Special sacrifices were also made at the graves of individual ancestors on the festivals of their births and deaths. Many families were able to trace their ancestry back for hundreds of years. Each new generation was therefore born into a stable community. The shrines of the ancestors represented the past; the newborn child represented the future. Once a man had sons who would burn incense on his grave he had no need to fear death. His life came from the earth and in due course it would return to the earth. As long as the spirits of the ancestors continued to be honoured, birth and death were part of that great cosmic order of which Kung Fu Tsu had spoken. The troubles of life could be borne with composure and the prospect of death faced with serenity. In her novel, *The Good Earth*, Pearl Buck described how the old Chinese peasant lived his last days in the ageless spirit of his ancestors.

> Spring passed and summer passed into harvest and in the hot autumn sun before winter comes Wang-Lung sat where his father had sat against the wall. And he thought no more about anything now except his food and his drink and his land. . . . And he was content holding it thus, and he thought of it fitfully and of his good coffin that was there, and the kind earth waited without haste until he came to it.

4 · A land of scholars

During the great days of the T'ang dynasty the soldiers of the Chinese Empire may well have met the soldiers of the Roman Empire on the plains of Asia. By the beginning of our era the Western empire had long since broken up under the barbarian invasions (Era 1, *Link*). China had also been overrun by invaders during the intervening centuries, yet, while the Roman Empire had fragmented into a large number of small states, China remained united. This was due to the strength of the ideas which we examined in the last chapter. But ideas need to be expressed in permanent form before they can act as a bond for men of differing types. Written language is therefore a cement for civilization.

It is generally assumed in the West that the Roman script is much more efficient than the cumbersome Chinese script. The letters of the Western alphabet are phonetic – that is, they are based on sounds made in speech – and they can therefore be kept to a limited number. Chinese characters, on the other hand, are symbols which represent the object being recorded. The

Chinese therefore need a vast number of characters, which have to be learned individually. The Western system has the advantage of simplicity. It has, however, one serious disadvantage. The members of every language group have to write the letters to suit the sounds of their own language, and therefore cannot read what is written by those who speak other tongues. When the barbarians swept over the Roman Empire, they adopted their own written languages. The problem was only partially solved by preserving Latin as a common language. The Roman type of script, therefore, tended to divide peoples from one another. When barbarians invaded the Chinese Empire, on the other hand, they had no difficulty in preserving their own languages, while writing in the common Chinese script. Thus, though the Chinese could not necessarily understand each other speak, they could read what each had written. This common written language had a powerful influence on keeping China a united people.

By the beginning of our era the technique of printing had been developed to a fine art. The earliest printing was done on silk or bamboo, but these

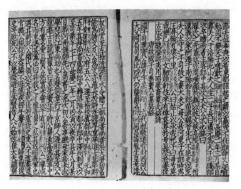

A Sung printed book

materials were expensive; so, as a cheap substitute, the Chinese had invented the material we call paper. By Sung times printing inks had been brought to a high level, and manufacturers had learnt to cover their paper with a fine glue or size to give it a smooth finish suitable for taking printing ink.

The Chinese did understand the technique of printing with movable type, which was to be re-invented by Gutenburg in the 15th Century (Era 4, page 37). This system was to prove ideal for printing in the simple Roman alphabet. It was, however, clearly impossible to use it effectively for the 40,000 symbols of the Chinese script. Printers continued to carve their pages from a single block.

Although the process was not mechanized, it was remarkably efficient. A professional scribe first wrote out a page on a piece of thin paper in the most elegant possible script. The block-maker meanwhile had prepared a block of wood, one side of which was planed smooth and finished off with size. He then placed the paper face downwards on the smooth surface of the block. When he peeled this paper off, the impression of the characters remained. The block-maker skilfully cut away the inked portions. He did this job so quickly that, if he made a mistake, it was generally simpler for him to plane down the face of the block and start again than to try to patch it up. The actual printing was carried out by hand, without a press, but a skilled man could produce up to 2,000 copies a day.

With so many characters to master, the sheer task of learning to read and write was daunting enough. Only children who showed unusual intelligence and tenacity of character could even embark on such a discipline. Pupils had to learn the different characters, and also how to draw them to the highest standard of perfection. By the time that the youngster could read and write he was already well schooled in the essential virtues of patience and diligence. He had not been asked to show any originality; only to reproduce what his master had shown him as exactly as possible.

In the course of time the local magistrates picked out those lads whom they considered fit to go on to higher levels of education at the provincial schools. Here they began the study of the traditional Confucian classics which would be their constant companions for many years. They had to learn to write essays commenting on these texts. The aspiring scholar was expected to mould his work as closely as possible to a standard pattern of perfection. Elegance of style was at least as important as accuracy of content. Even at the time there were some who protested at this system of training the young. They claimed that it placed too little emphasis on the development of ideas and tended to produce men who conformed uncritically to the ways of the past.

The imperial examination system was the gateway to the glory and the material rewards which were looked upon as the true deserts of the successful scholar. Every two, or later every three years, candidates gathered at the imperial capital to pit themselves against their rivals in one of the most exacting tests ever devised. Candidates subjected themselves to gruelling months of concentrated preparation to round off years of work aimed towards this one moment. They had already passed lesser tests, first in the district and then in the provincial capitals. Now they were aspiring to the greatest honour of all. No age limit was set on candidates, nor was there any restriction on the number of times which one man could sit. Some impatient young men sat the

Sung painting. A scholar
contemplates nature

exam when they were still in their early twenties; some dogged elders were still presenting themselves when they were seventy years old. The majority were probably around thirty-five.

Complex precautions were taken to ensure that all the proceedings were scrupulously fair. Papers were prepared in conditions of the greatest secrecy, and no examiner was allowed to know the name of the man whose work he was marking. A thousand or more candidates sat, cut off from each other in little booths, trying to produce the perfect 'eight legged' essay in the classical style. It was a severe test of each candidate's intelligence and memory, and also of his capacity to work under strain. Once again, however, it hardly provided any kind of test of his power of original thought; indeed originality would be more likely to have lost than to have gained marks.

At last, when the marking was finished, horsemen set out from the capital to carry the good news to those who had been successful. In the early days of the dynasty these would have been no more than a score or two, but by the end of the Sung period it was normal for over a hundred to pass. Many of these were the sons of scholars, and from childhood had had every opportunity to improve themselves. But the messengers also went out to poor homes where families had undergone years of sacrifice to allow their bright lads to achieve this ambition. These fortunate men would return to the capital, where they would be led through the streets by that most envied of all beings – the man who had come out top in the whole examination. A few weeks before, the successful candidate might have been so poor that he had to walk barefooted to the capital to sit his paper. Now he was a popular hero, admired by the young and looked upon as a suitable husband for the highest-born girl in the land.

In theory the candidate went to all this trouble for the opportunity which success gave for greater service to the community. But he was also able to look forward to a bright personal future. His position in society and the financial security of himself and his family were fully assured, for he was now admitted to the ranks of the *élite* scholar class to which was entrusted the government of the country.

In the early days of the Chinese Empire, power had lain with the feudal landowners, as it still did in medieval Europe. But the emperors had found that these men became independent of him, concerned with building up their own family fortunes. Over the centuries power had therefore been taken away from these feudal lords and given instead to those who succeeded in the imperial examinations. This had two advantages. In the first place the

28

country's rulers were bound to be able men. An old Confucian saying stressed the importance of recruiting talent into government service.

> When the right men are available, government flourishes;
> When the right men are not available, government declines.

The system had another important advantage. The men entrusted with responsibility had won their own way to the top. There was no kind of automatic succession, such as exists with a feudal aristocracy. The scholar rulers were therefore always the emperor's men. They owed their power to the throne, and in return gave the emperor all their loyalty. They also had strong financial inducements to remain loyal. Beyond their salaries, officials received

An official (Ming)

A scholar (Ming)

regular allowances of silk, cotton, rice, fuel, wine and tea. Those who served in the provinces were given grants of public land. It was traditional for emperors to be generous to their servants and the Sungs carried this to unprecedented lengths. One emperor left one million taels of silver to each of his ministers when he died. The Sungs also allowed more candidates to pass the examination, and consequently had to increase the number of official positions in order to accommodate them. By the end of our era, therefore,

29

these payments to imperial servants were becoming a serious drain on the resources of the state.

The gentleman scholar represented the highest ideal of Confucian manhood. His life was properly dedicated to the service of others so that he 'suffered before anyone suffered, and enjoyed himself after everyone had enjoyed themselves'. His mind was set on seeking after wisdom and his senses fixed on the most beautiful things in life. Ideally he was poet, a calligraphist, an artist as well as a profound Confucian scholar and a wise lawyer. He was expected to be good at chess and a master of the lute, and to have more than a passing knowledge of history, astronomy, music, languages, magic, and even mathematics and medicine. He might live in a lavish and splendid manner, or he might prefer the bare and frugal life, but, whatever his life-style, he was expected to show the characteristics of a true gentleman.

The ideal of the Chinese gentleman remained remarkably stable from the time of Kung Fu Tsu in the 6th Century BC down to the collapse of the Chinese Empire at the beginning of our own century (Era 9, Chapter 3). Traditions were consciously preserved. Many scholars preferred to dress in clothes modelled on those worn during the great days of the Han dynasty, rather than in the styles of their own time.

Although the influence of the past was strong, every period made its own particular contribution to civilization. The time of the Southern Sungs saw a rich flowering of Chinese culture. It was perhaps the greatest of all eras for poetry. It was also a period of studied elegance in written prose style. The Sung writer Su Shih described his own work in these words:

> My essays are like thousands of fountains shooting with a violent burst from an uncharted wilderness. When the water reaches the plain it becomes a roaring torrent, sweeping thousands of miles with complete ease. When it encounters rock and mountains, it changes its shape and course and adjusts itself to its surroundings. It is completely unpredictable. It goes whenever it should go and stops whenever it should stop.

This was also a great period for painting. The artist did not set out to copy nature; rather he used his brush to communicate those truths which lie below the surface of the visible world. The artist might spend days in the hills, looking at their beauty and trying to feel within himself that harmony which underlay all things, but he never painted in the open air. Alone in his room he would bring the images back to his mind and express them in paint.

The painter holds the brush steadily, looks intently at the paper, and visualizes the broadest outlines of the proposed painting. When the vision flashes, he follows it quickly, and, with his brush sweeping across the paper, he pursues it as a falcon chases an elusive rabbit. If he slackens his pace, his vision escapes and may never return.

Sung artists painted flowers, bamboo, birds and animals. Best known, however, are the landscapes which show mountains and rivers, men and animals all brought together into harmony.

The three great religious traditions of China – Confucianism, Taoism and Buddhism – are brought together and illustrated in the works of great Sung artists, like Ma Yuan.

a *Confucianism.* Following in the tradition of Kung Fu Tsu (see pages 16–17), the artist strove to give expression to the harmony which lies behind all things.

b *Taoism.* This ancient nature religion of China put man firmly in his place alongside other animate and inanimate objects of the world around him. According to the great Taoist teachers man has to stop looking upon himself as something apart from the rest of nature and learn to accept the round of birth and death, of joy and sorrow, without anxiety or resentment. Following this tradition the Sung painters showed human beings as tiny objects – paddling canoes, leading buffaloes or crossing bridges – utterly dwarfed by the mountains and waterfalls which surround them. Man is not overcome by the world of nature, but neither is he its master.

c *Buddhism.* (See Land of the Great Mogul, Chapter 4.) The religion of the Buddha came to China from India, bringing with it the discipline of meditation by which the human soul could find the peace of nirvana. The great Sung artists were able to express the silence of Buddhism. In particular they were not afraid to leave large areas of their pictures untouched in order to heighten the sense of stillness.

This combination of Buddhism with the older religions of China produced the distinctive philosophy of *Zen*, which reached its first peak in Sung times. This branch of Buddhism was later to develop yet further in Japan, but the greatest paintings of our era are looked upon as supreme expressions of the spirit of Zen.

Only the few who can read Chinese are able to enter fully into the literature

Landscape by Sung artist Yen Tz'u-yu shows the insignificance of man against the background of nature and the use of empty spaces to portray stillness

and poetry of that great civilization. The philosophy of Zen in particular is elusive and hard to understand. But painting does not need an interpreter. From the works of the artists we are able in some measure to penetrate the ways of thought of those cultured scholars who set the tone for society and brought their awareness of the beautiful and their love of learning to such a high pitch of excellence.

5 · *The City of Heaven*

Members of the scholar aristocracy might be asked to serve their emperor in any part of his dominions. During the period of the Southern Sungs, however, their true home was the capital city of Hanchow. Here men of learning could meet to share their enthusiasms for the beautiful things of life. Here they could share in the elegant life of the court and wait upon the emperor himself.

We have seen (page 17) that Hanchow only rose to importance after the disasters of the Chin invasion, which culminated in the fall of Kaifeng in 1126. The Emperor Kao Tsung, founder of Southern Sung, chose it as his capital because it could be defended against the raiding horsemen from the north. For many years, it was reported, in rainy weather officials waded through deep mud which lay in the streets of this makeshift capital. Courtiers did not want to make themselves too much at home, for then they would forget the lost provinces and the old capital city, which lay in barbarian hands. In the course of time, however, they had to come to terms with reality. Slowly Hanchow began to look like the seat of the greatest ruler on earth. The royal palaces never quite attained the standard of those lost in Kaifeng; the triumphal roads were never so wide or imposing. Yet Hanchow had a greatness of its own, for it developed a unique combination of commercial prosperity, typical of the great cities of the south, with the pomp and pageantry of an imperial capital. By the end of its century-and-a-half of glory it had grown to be a city of well over a million inhabitants.

Kao Tsung may have been thinking mainly of defence when he chose Hanchow as his capital, but the site had other important advantages.

Situated half way between the Yangtze River and the coast, it was well placed to become an important commercial centre. Also, ringed by hills and beside a clear lake, it had a breathtakingly beautiful setting. We are fortunate in being able to reconstruct a picture of the city and the life of the people in reasonable detail. There are many important Chinese sources, which have been studied by scholars, and these are supplemented by a long description in

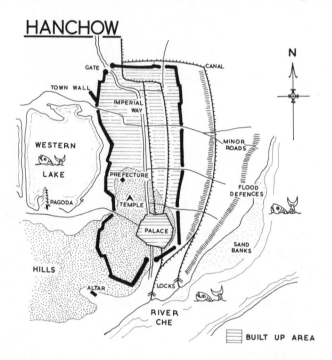

HANCHOW

the journal of Marco Polo, who visited the city shortly after the fall of the Sung emperors. Marco Polo was deeply impressed by Hanchow, which he called Kinsai – the City of Heaven. Its size, the skills of its people, the quality of its life, dwarfed anything that he had seen in Europe. Explorers like Columbus and Cabot who, more than two centuries later, set off to find this distant land, had their imaginations fired by the description that he had left.

The first impression given by Hanchow to the Venetian traveller was of size and spaciousness. Yet, despite its size, the streets were clean, the water was fresh, and the air was not fouled with the smell of putrefying animal and vegetable matter, universal in European cities of the period.

34

夜語重門休上鑰
夜潮留向月中看

Hanchow bay by moonlight by Sung artist Li Sung.
(Note construction of houses with wooden pillars and curved roofs.)

35

The city of Kinsai is about 100 miles in circumference, because its streets and watercourses are wide and spacious. Then there are market-places, which because of the multitudes that throng them must be very large and spacious. The lay-out of the city is as follows. On one side is a lake of fresh water, very clear. On the other is a huge river, which entering by many channels, diffused throughout the city, carries away all its filth and then flows into the lake, from which it flows out towards the Ocean. This makes the air very wholesome. And through every part of the city it is possible to travel either by land or by these streams. The streets and the watercourses alike are very wide, so that carts and boats can readily pass along them to carry provisions for the inhabitants. There are said to be 12,000 bridges, mostly of stone, though some are of wood. Those over the main channels and the chief thoroughfare are built with such lofty arches and so well designed that big ships can pass under them without a mast, and yet over them pass carts and horses; so well are the street-levels adjusted to the height. Under the other bridges smaller craft can pass. No one need be surprised that there are so many bridges. For the whole city lies in water and surrounded by water, so that many bridges are needed to let people go all over the town.

The Travels of Marco Polo, Penguin, pp. 213–14.

A description by a Chinese writer gives a similar impression, though with a sharper awareness of the beauty of the scene.

Green mountains surround on all sides the still waters of the lake. Pavilions and towers in hues of gold and azure rise here and there. One would say, a landscape composed by a painter. Only towards the east, where there are no hills, does the land open out, and there sparkle, like fishes' scales, the light coloured tiles of a thousand roofs.

It is fortunate that writers have left such descriptions, for little evidence of the old city remains underground to be investigated by archaeologists. The great buildings of Europe, from the earliest civilizations, have been constructed in stone, and the evidence of the past can never be wholly destroyed. Even the palaces of China were built of wood which in time rots away to nothing.

The main structure of the houses was formed by wooden pillars, set on stone supports about three yards apart. The area between these supports was filled in with bamboo screenwork or a thin layer of brick. In the countryside, houses were rarely built above a single storey high. But building land was precious in Hanchow and houses in the city were therefore built several storeys high.

The crowning glory of a Chinese house was its roof, which rested on the main wooden supports which formed the framework of the building. It was made of tiles – jade green, pale green or yellow – to tone in with the colours of the hills and the trees. It had also become the fashion among the richer folk to have their roofs curved, again so that they would match the rounded shapes in nature.

The homes of the wealthy were to be found in the southern suburbs. Their owners spared no expense to provide themselves with a worthy setting in which to live the good life. These houses were set in elegant grounds, which in season blazed with many-coloured flowers and trees, heavy with blossom. Streams were diverted to form miniature waterfalls, and artificial lakes reflected the shapes of elegant summerhouses.

Houses made of wood and bamboo burnt very easily, and fire was one of the major hazards of life in the capital. Once it caught hold in the crowded areas, it could spread with frightening speed. Careful precautions were

A fire tower. (Han)

therefore taken to ensure that the swiftest possible warning was given of any outbreak. Every 500 yards there were guard stations with watchtowers from which watchmen could scan the city by day and night. At the first sign of trouble they gave signals to indicate precisely where the blaze had broken out. Soon a hundred trained fire-fighters, who were continually standing by, were at the scene. Despite all precautions, however, fires often did get out of control. On one occasion over 50,000 houses were destroyed in a terrible conflagration, which lasted for four days. Fifty-nine people were known to have been burnt to death and many more were trampled underfoot as the people stampeded for the city gates.

When a fire was over the emperor would do his best to help the distress of those who had lost their homes. Taxes and rents were waived and food was given to those in need. Yet the emperor could not disclaim responsibility for what had happened. As representative of Heaven, it was his task to avert the anger of the elements. After one particularly disastrous fire had rendered tens of thousands of citizens homeless, the emperor of the day imposed proper punishment on himself, by confining himself to his apartment and cutting out all luxuries from his life.

Following traditional Chinese practice, all occupations were organized into an elaborate network of guilds, which provided a structure of local government for the city. Marco Polo, himself accustomed to the guild system in the West, was impressed by the size and power of these organizations.

> The city was organized in twelve main guilds, one for each craft, not to speak of the many lesser ones. Each of these twelve guilds had 12,000 establishments, that is to say 12,000 workshops, each employing at least ten men and some as many as forty. I do not mean that they were all masters, but men working under the command of masters.
>
> *The Travels of Marco Polo*, p. 217.

Every occupation had its own guild, from doctors to scavengers. Each vied with the others to find the most impressive-sounding name. Keepers of public bathing houses, for instance, rejoiced in the title of 'companions of the fragrant water'.

As in the West, the guilds existed to limit competition so that the living standards of those who depended on a particular trade for their livelihood could be preserved. Regulations established standards of craftsmanship, and minimum – but not maximum – prices at which goods could be sold. They further laid down rules about weights and measures, relationships between master and servant, and also controlled problems over credit and bankruptcy.

Most of the day-to-day problems of life could be settled within the guild structure. If a dispute occurred between members of the same guild, it would be judged by their own arbitration committee. If the dispute lay between members of different guilds, then members of a third guild would be called in to judge between them. Imperial officials were therefore forced to treat the guilds with great respect. If the guild councils ceased to co-operate, then the even tenor of life was immediately disrupted.

The trades were carried on in small workshops, in which goods were both manufactured and sold. A master would be assisted in his trade by a small number of apprentices and workmen. The relationship between master and servant was strictly controlled by the Confucian code of conduct. Generally speaking trade was conducted in a spirit of mutual trust. In any transaction, a man's word was considered to be enough without written confirmation.

Vase showing a potter's workshop (17th–18th Century)

Hanchow was a city of bustling activity. Late into the evening the broad Imperial Way, which led to the gateway of the emperor's palace, would be crowded with people, busy buying and selling. Yet at the same time it was remarkably peaceful. Marco Polo, accustomed to the robust Italian city life, was amazed at the sense of general goodwill.

The natives of Kinsai are men of peace, through being so cosseted and pampered by their kings, who were of the same temper. They have no skill in handling arms and do not keep any in their houses. There is prevalent among them a dislike and distaste for strife or any sort of disagreement. They pursue their trades and handicrafts with great diligence and honesty. They love one another so devotedly that a whole district might seem, from the friendly and neighbourly spirit that rules among men and women, to be a single household.

The Travels of Marco Polo, p. 219.

Yet no city of such proportions could be entirely without problems of law and order. Bands of thieves – themselves organized into guilds – operated in the maze of little streets which lay behind the broad main thoroughfares. It was never easy for a law-abiding citizen to protect his property, for though he might lock his door at night, it was all too simple for the robbers to break through the flimsy bamboo or brick screenwork which filled the gaps between the main supports of the house.

The population of the city more than doubled in the century from 1175 to 1275. Since there was little space for building on the outskirts, the city itself became increasingly crowded. Every month more peasants arrived from the countryside, hoping to find a better life than they had known in their villages. These newcomers would be happy to find even the most menial employment. Some worked as labourers, keeping the roads in repair or clearing silt from the lake and canals. Some drew clear water from the lake and sold it from door to door. Many found employment hawking their wares around the streets of the city. A surprisingly large number gained their living from the Chinese habit of indulging their children's whims. Boys and girls worried their parents for a few coins when they heard the cry of the sweet seller, who carried sticks of sugar-cane and little animals and people made out of sugar. They also stared in wonder at the toy sellers who walked the streets with large bamboo frameworks strapped to their backs, from which dangled scores of brightly painted dolls and toys of all kinds.

There were also jobs to be found in the homes of the rich, where vast numbers of servants tended the houses and gardens. The man who had any special skill in riding a horse, dancing, playing chess, making up riddles, training performing insects, arranging animal fights, telling stories, playing a musical instrument, handling marionettes, or performing acrobatics, might hope to find secure employment in one of the large houses. Those who were not so fortunate, made what livings they could on the streets as wandering entertainers. The people of Hanchow loved to be entertained. Crowds clustered round the storytellers as they gave vivid accounts of the tribulations of poor scholars, of ancient battles, or told fantastic tales of demons and genies. They also watched actors perform the traditional dramas, marionettes dance jerkily on their little stage, and shadow plays performed by puppets cut out of paper. They liked to hold their breath as tight-rope walkers performed wonderful feats of balance, holding jars full of water, high above the street. They watched, too, with admiration as acrobats twisted their bodies until they walked with their heads thrust between their legs.

More serious men from the north frowned upon the tireless search of the southern Chinese for pleasure. If there was an occasion to celebrate – such as a birth or marriage – a father might choose to take his family boating on the lake. Marco Polo marvelled at the elegance of that scene.

> The lake is provided with a great number of boats or barges, big and small, in which the people take pleasure-trips for the sake of recreation. These will hold ten, fifteen, twenty or more persons, as they range from

Boating scene (14th Century)

> fifteen to twenty paces in length and are flat-bottomed and broad in the beam, so as to float without rocking. Anyone who likes to enjoy himself with female society or with his boon companions hires one of these barges, which are kept continually furnished with fine seats and tables and all the other requisites for a party. They are roofed over with decks

41

on which stand men with poles which they thrust into the bottom of the lake (for it is not more than two paces in depth) and thus propel the barges where they are bidden. The deck is painted inside with various colours and designs and so is the whole barge, and all round it are windows that can be shut or opened so that the banqueters ranged along the sides can look this way and that and feast their eyes on the diversity and beauty of the scenes through which they are passing. And indeed a voyage on this lake offers more refreshment and delectation than any other experience on earth.

The Travels of Marco Polo, pp. 218–19.

On a fine night the surface of the water reflected the light of hundreds of lanterns tied in the bows and sterns of these little craft, with the hills behind outlined against the night sky.

A family might prefer to go to one of the pavilions which specialized in providing banquets, with all the trimmings proper to such a celebration; or, on less formal occasions, to one of the city's many restaurants. Visitors to the city wondered at the bewildering variety of food served.

The people of Hanchow are very difficult to please. Hundreds of orders are given on all sides; this person wants something hot, another something cold, a third something tepid, a fourth something chilled; one wants cooked food, another raw, another chooses roast, another grilled. The orders, given in a loud voice, are all different, sometimes three different ones at the same table.

If a man was looking for quiet conversation, without a heavy meal, he could visit a tea house. These had a restful atmosphere, enhanced by beautiful flowers, evergreen trees, and tasteful decorations. Well-mannered girls moved here and there serving tea in fine porcelain dishes off brightly lacquered trays, while customers talked over the affairs of the city or conducted business in an unhurried manner.

If the mood of the moment demanded something stronger than tea, there was also a wide variety of taverns. They offered rice wines of differing flavours, which could be taken with pies made of pork, mutton, shrimp or silkworms. Some were elegant establishments, where the decorations were in good taste and the company quiet. Others, decorated with garish blinds and brightly coloured lanterns, were intended to provide the setting for a more boisterous evening's entertainment.

42

Perhaps an even stronger attraction than the wine, the food and the decorations were the beautiful girls who graced the taverns. Once again, the role which they fulfilled tended to vary with the 'tone' of the establishment. Like the geishas of Japan, these young ladies were highly skilled in giving

A lady with a mirror (T'ang)

pleasure to men. When recording the experiences of his travels in China, Marco Polo remembered them with a special tenderness.

> These ladies are highly proficient and accomplished in the uses of endearments and caresses, with words suited and adapted to every sort of person, so that foreigners who have once enjoyed them remain utterly beside themselves and so captivated by their sweetness and charm that they can never forget them. So it comes about that, when they return home, they say they have been in 'Kinsai', that is to say the city of Heaven, and can scarcely wait for the time when they may go back there.
>
> *The Travels of Marco Polo*, p. 216.

They provided a contrast to the more respectable women who stayed at home while their men went out to the taverns. These wives and mothers were well bred, quiet and self-effacing. Each type of woman had her role to fulfil within society, and neither was without her own brand of honour.

Morning in the Palace,
by Sung artist Chao Po-chü

A stoneware pillow.
This illustrates the Chinese tendency
to stress elegance rather than comfort. (Sung)

The whole city took its tone from the court of the Emperor of Heaven. The Palace of the Refreshing Spring was set on a hill so that it was always fanned by cool breezes. The Palace of Coolness was constructed out of ivory-white Japanese pinewood. In its grounds were set hundreds of urns containing the blossoms of jasmine, orchids and all kinds of exotic shrubs. These were fanned by a windmill so that the fragrance could be spread across the garden.

The Emperor's dragon robe
(19th Century, copied from an ancient pattern)

The walls of the hall were lined with bronze receptacles containing snow, perfumes, fruit and sugar-cane juice. The air indoors was heavy with the perfume of burning incense and plump yellow-and-white cats nestled on rich cushions. A modern visitor would certainly consider that far too little effort had been put into making the palaces comfortable, in comparison with that

45

which had gone into making them beautiful. Although winters could be cold, nobody had invented a satisfactory method of heating the large rooms. Furniture was also sparse and uncomfortable. Yet, compared with the bare, stone keeps of Europe, they provided luxury indeed.

Closest around the emperor were the princes of the royal blood and the women of the palace – empress, dowager empress, and concubines. This privileged group was generally divorced from the realities of life, and split by faction, and all too often the emperor himself was almost a prisoner of one group or other. Beyond this inner circle there were, it is estimated, over 10,000 scholar families who, to a greater or lesser degree, lived off the court. As in all such communities, a great deal of time and effort was expended on the formalities of life – dress, food and etiquette.

In view of the inadequate heating, dress had to be functional as well as ornamental. Robes used in winter were lined with fur or silk floss to protect the wearer against the cold. By tradition, the colour and style of clothes depended on the position of the wearer and those with a practised eye could gauge the status of a courtier by the shape of his head-dress and the style of his girdle. Even the humblest Chinese covered his head and wore a girdle at his waist, for these were the signs which distinguished a civilized man from a barbarian. Perfumes, cosmetics and jewellery enhanced the beauty of women of rank. Chinese men liked their women-folk to be small and delicate. The custom of foot-binding, introduced in the 10th Century, was rapidly gaining in favour. Girls' feet were tightly encased in bandages during their growing period, so that women could have the delicate feet of a child. Women whose feet had been deformed in this way, could only hobble with tiny steps. This was, however, looked upon as the proper way for a lady of rank to walk. The practice continued into our own century. In different societies women have suffered much in the cause of fashion, but no male fancy can have caused so much suffering as the custom of foot-binding.

Courtiers ate lavishly, although the stress was always laid on the variety and quality of the food offered rather than on mere quantity. A menu at the emperor's table might include scented shellfish cooked in rice wine, goose with apricots, lotus seed soup, pimento soup with mussels and delicate soufflées of all kinds. The food was cut in small pieces so that it could be eaten with chopsticks and spoons, and was served on low tables. Drinking tea was also as important an activity among courtiers as it was in other ranks of society. The whole atmosphere at court was unhurried, elegant and restrained. The finest painters, poets, flower arrangers and calligraphers all combined their skills to make the environment as perfect as could be achieved by man.

The emperor was looked upon by his subjects as the Son of Heaven, a semi-divine creature, far apart from the everyday life of common people. The routine and the beauty of the court all helped to preserve this image, upon which the sense of security of all the people was based. Behind the façade of court life a reasonably efficient administrative system ran the nation's life. Government departments issued imperial edicts and courts dispensed justice, but, to ordinary people, the machinery of government was less important than the aura which surrounded the person of the emperor.

Emperor and people came together at the times of the great sacrifices and

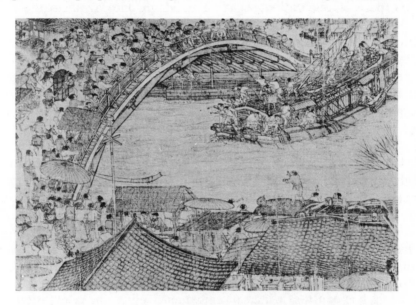

Spring Festival on the river, by Chang Tse Tuan (detail). The Northern Sung artist shows Kaifeng at festival time. (Note the tea house by the canal bank and the mast of the barge being lowered to pass under the bridge.)

festivals, when the whole city was gripped in a mood of festivity. Best loved were the celebrations to greet the New Year. On the last days of the old year the restaurants of the city were busy serving family banquets. Gradually the mood built up until New Year's Eve, 'the end of the moons and the last day of the year'. Then the old images of the gods which had guarded the doorway of every house during the past year were taken down and the image of Chung K'uei, the demon-tamer, decked with gaily coloured streamers, was hung up instead. As night fell each family went indoors to offer sacrifices to the gods of the door, bed, stove and courtyard. Away in the imperial palace the father of his people went through the same routine on behalf of his huge family. When the sacrifices were completed a procession emerged from the doors of the palace. Masked courtiers, carrying gilded staffs, wooden swords and coloured flags, toured the streets 'chasing pestilences' from the city.

On New Year's Day, at dawn, the emperor, in the presence of his officials, burnt incense to the Lord of Heaven, seeking good crops for his people in the coming year. For the next three days everyone stayed quietly at home. After that the pace of celebration began to build up once again to the climax provided by the Feast of Lanterns which fell at full moon in the first lunar month of the year. Then Hanchow burst into a blaze of colour. The doors and windows of all the houses – from the emperor's palace to the homes of the very poorest – were draped with gaily coloured curtains. Lanterns, large and small, hung everywhere; some shaped like boats or dragons, some constantly turning by means of water power, some decorated by paintings, some inlaid with semi-precious stones. Scholar officials came into the streets arrayed in gorgeous robes of silk or brocade decorated with weird dragons. Rich and poor jostled one another in the streets, each carrying his own lantern over his shoulder. Bands of musicians played while professional dancers displayed their skill. The whole city was like a bonfire, and, in view of the combustible nature of the buildings, it was a constant wonder that Hanchow did not indeed become a bonfire every New Year.

Whatever other failings they may have had, the people of Hanchow certainly knew the secret of enjoying themselves. Perhaps Marco Polo was right in thinking that they had become soft in the process. Yet life was far from being one constant round of enjoyment. When the celebrations were over, master and servant had to return to their work so that they could earn the money with which to enjoy the good things of life.

6 · Village life

It was not the cities, like Hanchow, but the thousands of small villages which dotted the countryside, that formed the basic unit of Chinese civilization. It was in particular in the villages that the pattern of family life, on which society rested, could be most clearly seen.

In modern, Western societies, the word 'family' is used to describe the small unit comprising parents and children, living in a house of its own. In China these two generations were never looked upon in isolation, for the family, or *chia*, included all living generations – grandparents, uncles, aunts and cousins – as well as the spirits of dead ancestors. This extended family provided the framework and the security for the lives of each of its members. The smallest child and the most helpless old person had an absolute right to the support of the family. A young man could leave home to try to improve his fortunes in the city, but, if things went badly, he could return, confident that he would not be turned away. The family provided the rising generation with standards of behaviour and a set of values by which to live. In its ancestor worship and sacrifices to the kitchen gods, it also provided the religious framework for existence.

All property belonged to the group as a whole. Nothing could therefore be sold without the consent of the head of the family, and even he could not take decisions without the support of the male elders. No one therefore worked for his own advantage, but for the prosperity of the whole group. Obviously families could not go on growing for ever, and so on occasions one chia split into two. Sometimes this would happen as a result of a quarrel within the family, sometimes from a mutual agreement that it was necessary to make the group smaller for everyone's convenience. Two brothers would then set up as heads of their own respective families, each with his own share of the family property. If the chia was reasonably wealthy, one of the brothers would build a new home for himself. It was quite common, however, for poorer families to remain under one roof even after the chias had split. In these circumstances the front room of the house would be divided and there would be two kitchen shrines instead of one.

The divided chias would remain members of a single clan. It was unusual for a village to have more than two or three clans, and in many villages there

THE PEASANT'S YEAR

JANUARY — MARCH

MUCH RICE ⊛   SOME RICE ◯

RICE GROWING IN CHINA

MAY — JUNE
THE SEEDS ARE SOWN IN THE NURSERY BEDS WHICH HAVE BEEN THOROUGHLY PREPARED.

WHILE THE PLANTS GROW THE MAIN FIELDS ARE FLOODED AND PLOUGHED.

JUNE — JULY

JULY — MID OCTOBER
THE RICE PLANTS ARE LEFT TO BLOSSOM, BEAR FRUIT AND RIPEN IN THE SMALL FLAT FIELDS.

THIS IS A QUIET TIME FOR THE FARMER.

MID OCTOBER — DECEMBER

THIS IS A QUIET PERIOD FOR THE FARMER, IT IS A TIME OF CELEBRATIONS AND VISITS OF RELATIVES.

THE CHINESE NEW YEAR IS CELEBRATED AT THE BEGINNING OF FEBRUARY.

THE SEEDLINGS ARE NOW TRANSPLANTED, THIS IS A VERY BUSY PERIOD FOR THE FARMER.

CONSTANT WEEDING AND IRRIGATION HAS TO BE DONE AT THIS STAGE.

THIS IS THE SECOND BUSY PERIOD FOR THE FARMER, THE RICE IS REAPED AND HUSKED.

SOME OF THE RICE IS STORED FOR FOOD AND SEED THE REST IS SOLD

APRIL — MAY
THE EGGS HATCH, THE COCOON IS FORMED.

THE MAIN CROP IS NOW HARVESTED.

JUNE
THE COCOONS ARE SOAKED AND REELED IN THE HOME.

JULY
THE SECOND CROP IS HARVESTED.

was only one. Like the families, these clans had a head, who was advised by the male elders. When there was more than one clan in a village, each sent a representative to serve on a council which was the governing body of the community. In single-clan villages the clan structure itself provided all necessary local government.

Day-to-day problems were dealt with entirely within the village community. Family heads settled problems within their own chias. If disputes arose between members of different chias, representatives of the families would be brought together by the clan head or village council so that they could thrash out their differences. Another code of laws existed, set up by the emperor and administered by his scholar officials, but simple people rarely had recourse to these exalted courts. A village managed its own affairs, and an imperial administrator was considered successful if he allowed this age-old structure to function undisturbed. These informal gatherings of elders were also responsible for important matters such as preserving the proper ancestor worship and choosing the boys who would be educated.

Naturally, when a village lad was picked to go to school, everyone hoped that one day he would bring honour to his village by passing the imperial examination. But the harsh fact was that only a tiny proportion achieved this distant goal. The majority failed one or other of the examinations along the way. These 'failed graduates' became a lower *élite* within the villages, without official status, but natural leaders of their communities.

As in all peasant societies, life followed an ordered cycle, closely geared to the changing seasons. We have seen (Chapter 1) that the way of life differed in the highlands and the lowlands; in the north and in the south. Some areas got their basic food from crops such as wheat and millet. Some, on the edges of the barbarian country, drew their livelihood from hunting or herding animals. We shall, however, look at the normal pattern of life in a village on the low-lying eastern plains, where the people depended on rice for the bulk of their diet and their main money-making activity was the raising of silkworms.

A visitor from the West would have noticed that there were very few animals in and around the village. A few pigs and chickens might be found, scavenging for food among the refuse, but cattle and goats, which could have provided meat and dairy produce for the people, were rare indeed. With the large population of the country, most of the land had to be given over to grain crops. There was also a traditional prejudice against dairy farming, which has lingered on into our own times. One result of this was that the people's diet was not well balanced, lacking calcium in particular. Secondly,

51

Rice farming in lowland China: irrigated fields

Rice farming in lowland China: terraced fields

there was little good manure for the soil. The villagers did what they could to get over this by carefully preserving all human waste and by scooping the mud from the bottom of ponds.

The survival of the villages depended on the success of the rice crop. The whole countryside was covered with a network of irrigation canals so that, when the rains came, the precious water could be used to the very best advantage. As far as possible the force of gravity was used to take the water where it was needed. But in places it had to be transported uphill by means of pumps, which the farmers worked with their feet. This involved hours of the most back-breaking work. Fields had to be flat, so that the water would lie on the surface of the soil. This meant that uneven land had to be laboriously levelled and the hillsides laid out in neat terraces.

The first busy farming season began in late May or early June, when the men started to prepare the soil of the nursery farm. Once the seed was safely planted in the nursery farm, the men had to prepare the main fields to receive the young shoots when they were ready to be transplanted. Then the water had to be pumped from the irrigation channels into the fields. At last, by the end of June, the main fields would be ready. Meanwhile the seeds in the nursery farm would have sprouted strong, green shoots. When all was ready, the young plants were lifted and brought to the main fields, where they were to grow to maturity. Transplanting rice for hours on end can be a back-breaking business, but the people lightened their task by working as a team. The boys handed the shoots to their elders, who planted them in the ground, their bodies moving in a swinging rhythm.

The first period of heavy labour was then over. Through July the rice grew, until in August the blossom appeared. At last, in September, the fruit began to form. During this period there was still plenty to keep the men occupied. If the rains stopped and the soil began to dry out, they had to start working the irrigation pumps once again. They also had to keep the fields free of weeds. They did this by dragging a plate with nails on one side, attached to a bamboo pole, across the soil between the rows of plants.

By late October the rice was ready to harvest, and the second period of hard work began. First the plants were cut off near the base of the stalk and tied into bundles, which were then carried to the front of the house. The family home was then turned into a factory for the hard work of threshing the seeds out of the husks. When at last the crop was gathered it had to be divided out. A proportion was put on one side to meet the demands of the tax gatherer. Then an assessment had to be made of how much the family would need to carry it through until the next harvest. Any surplus would be taken to market to be exchanged for the precious coins which would buy a few luxuries during the coming year. If the harvest was good there would be enough for all three purposes, but if the crops were poor there would be none to spare to take to market and the people would beg the tax man to be merciful to them. In bad years peasants had to take desperate measures in order to stay alive.

Some sold their farms to moneylenders from the towns, and from that time onwards had to hand over a large part of their produce every year as rent. Some sold their children as slaves in the hope that they would be adopted by a rich family and so grow up in a comfort their own parents could not afford to give them.

Preparing the rice crop.
At the rear: husking
Left to right: winnowing, sieving, pounding

In China farming was always looked upon as men's work. The women made their contribution to the family by tending the house and looking after the silkworms which brought in a valuable second income. The higher land, above the irrigation level, was used for the cultivation of the mulberry trees essential to the silk industry. In April adult moths laid their eggs on the leaves of the mulberry trees. The women and girls would then carefully collect these eggs and lay them out on trays, which were brought into the house and kept warm until the eggs hatched out and the young silkworms appeared. These were carefully tended until, at the end of May, they began to spin their precious cocoon. At last the new generation of moths would emerge and leave the women to gather up their rejected shelters.

54

Details from a scroll by the Sung emperor Hui Tsung (see page 15)

Women winding and beating newly woven silk

All through June, while the men were sowing the seed in the fields, the women were busy spinning and reeling the fine thread, and preparing for the second silk crop, which would be ready at the beginning of July. Once all the moths had flown away, the women were able to work at their own pace on the endless tasks of spinning, reeling and weaving. Some of the cloth was kept for the use of the family; the rest would be taken to market. Ultimately it would find its way to the cities, and even to market-places as far away as Western Europe.

For both the men who tilled the fields and the women who produced the silk, work was therefore concentrated into certain busy seasons. During these periods the members of the family had to shift for themselves as best they could as most of the rooms in the house would be given over to trays of squirming silkworms or piles of rice brought in from the fields. During these periods nobody had any time to do more than offer hurried sacrifices to the kitchen god, whose duty was to watch over the daily life of the home, and to make regular reports to the Emperor of Heaven.

During slack times, however, the villagers had more leisure. The rejoicing feasts of Chung Ch'iu and Chung Yang fell during the period when the rice was ripening in the fields, after the women had gathered the second silk crop. The long New Year celebrations came in the slack winter months. While the emperor and citizens of Hanchow were celebrating, the villagers kept the festival in their own more modest way. By tradition the first month of the year was an auspicious time for weddings, and so there were likely to be celebrations all through the month. Then, by mid-March, people began to think of the more serious side of life once again. The tombs of the ancestors had to be visited so that a report could be given on the progress of the family; sacrifices had to be made to the god of silkworms, before the moths began to lay the new season's eggs in the mulberry trees; and there was work to be done, preparing the house and farm for another busy season.

Although the tide of work rose and fell with the seasons, no time was completely slack. Since there was little meat to be had, the people relied largely on fish to provide protein for their diet. In the summer the men fished the rivers with nets and hooks. During the winter, when smaller watercourses were reduced to a trickle, the men dragged hooks through the mud to catch the fish that were hibernating there. Anyone who eats a Chinese meal today will notice that the methods of cooking are designed to help a small amount of fish or meat go a long way. We can be sure that villagers through the centuries have

Vase showing fishermen

Model of a granary

eaten far less protein than is served to a Western customer in a Chinese restaurant today.

The Chinese dependence on cereal crops was directly related to the pressure of population. It takes ten times as much land to graze enough animals to provide a meat diet for a given number of people, as it takes to feed the same number of people on a plant diet. Population was densest in those areas in the south where the warm climate permitted farmers to take two, or even three, rice crops from their fields in a single year. As in all peasant communities, the margin between plenty and hunger, between life and death, was a narrow one. As long as the rains fell when expected; as long as the river stayed within its banks; as long as the locusts stayed away; as long as disease did not strike at the young silkworms: then life was tolerable and men could believe with Kung Fu Tsu that man was in harmony with nature. Old men could then go to their graves, content in the knowledge that the family lands had been preserved intact and the traditions of the ancestors had been handed on to the rising generation.

7 · The wealth of China

China was not a unified nation, in the sense that Europeans have understood the term in the past four centuries, but rather a collection of cells, each of which had a life of its own, independent of its neighbours. Each cell consisted of a large city with an area of countryside around it: town and country together formed a self-contained unit. The countrymen provided food, wood, silk and other essential supplies for the town dwellers. In return they received money for the goods which they sold and also such measure of protection as could be afforded by the city's walls. As long as life continued quietly, the officials interfered as little as possible, for fear of upsetting the delicate balance.

This system had advantages as well as disadvantages. On the credit side, trouble tended to remain localized. If the barbarians invaded they might bring death and starvation to the people in a few provinces, but this did not upset

Model of a bullock cart. (T'ang)

Model boat (Ming)

the lives of those beyond their reach. On the debit side, when famine broke out in an area, it was very hard to organize the rapid transport of food to bring relief.

When Marco Polo saw the crowds milling on the Imperial Way in Hanchow, he wondered how so many mouths could possibly be fed. Indeed the existence of such large cities had an enormous influence on the economic life of the nation. In a purely subsistence economy peasants have little incentive to produce more than is needed to supply their own immediate needs. But the very existence of cities depends on the ability of farmers to produce a surplus. There was therefore a huge trade between town and country.

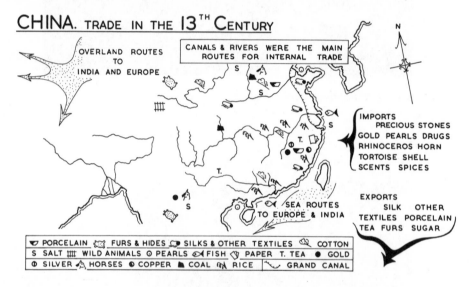

CHINA. TRADE IN THE 13TH CENTURY

OVERLAND ROUTES TO INDIA AND EUROPE

CANALS & RIVERS WERE THE MAIN ROUTES FOR INTERNAL TRADE

IMPORTS
PRECIOUS STONES GOLD PEARLS DRUGS RHINOCEROS HORN TORTOISE SHELL SCENTS SPICES

EXPORTS
SILK OTHER TEXTILES PORCELAIN TEA FURS SUGAR

SEA ROUTES TO EUROPE & INDIA

PORCELAIN   FURS & HIDES   SILKS & OTHER TEXTILES   COTTON
S SALT   WILD ANIMALS   O PEARLS   FISH   PAPER   T. TEA   ● GOLD
SILVER   HORSES   COPPER   ■ COAL   RICE   GRAND CANAL

Marco Polo, indeed, saw ample evidence of this trade. All day long and far into the night carts rumbled along the roads which led from outlying villages into the city. There was also an elaborate network of canals in which goods could be shifted in bulk. Most of this local trade was in basic items, such as grain and fuel. Huge quantities of rice, in particular, were brought into Hanchow to be unloaded at the rice markets, where it was bought by shop-keepers and the owners of restaurants. There was also a lively trade in pork, fish, fruit, olives, herbs and all the raw materials needed by the different craftsmen to enable them to carry out their trades.

A large part of the money earned by peasant farmers through this trade

60

had to be kept back to meet the imperial tax demands. The gain was not, however, all on one side. The fact that the villages were able to pay taxes at all meant that the state had money available to keep dykes and canals in good repair. Also, with the surplus left after taxes were paid, villagers were able to buy manufactured goods from the towns, such as kitchen bowls and farming implements, which did much to make their lives more tolerable.

Most of China's trade consisted of this two-way traffic between town and countryside, but, owing to shortages of natural resources in some areas, certain commodities had to be transported longer distances. It is estimated that almost a million people lived in semi-slavery, working the government salt beds in the Huai Marshes in the south-east. Marco Polo noticed that a large proportion of the country's trade was in salt. Other commodities which often had to cross provincial boundaries were iron, hemp and – owing to the deforestation of large areas of the country – wood and charcoal. There was also a small but important luxury trade. Loyang in the north and Yueh in the south were particularly noted for producing fine-quality ceramics, which were valued by people of taste in all parts of the country, and certain specific areas were noted for the fine quality of their tea.

A large proportion of the trade, both short and long distance, was carried on the country's extensive network of rivers and canals. Marco Polo commented with astonishment on the volume of traffic on the Yangtze River.

> On its banks are innumerable cities and towns, and the amount of shipping it carries and the bulk of merchandise that merchants transport by it, upstream and down, is so inconceivable that no one in the world who had not seen it with his own eyes could possibly credit it.
>
> *The Travels of Marco Polo*, p. 170.

The Grand Canal provided an invaluable link between the north and the south, crossing the rivers as they flowed eastwards towards the sea. This great engineering work, which dated from the 7th Century AD, stretched 1,000 miles, from Hanchow in the south to Peking in the north. Forty paces wide, it was shaded by willows and had state highways on its banks. The Grand Canal was a powerful influence in uniting the culture of the north and south, through the passage of trading goods and the ideas which went with them.

Merchants always ran the risk of being attacked by brigands along the way, and trading parties were often provided with a military escort. One merchant described how his party travelled through the night.

The moon was so bright that everything was as clear as daylight. The escorting soldiers, full of courage, called out to each other from one boat to another all through the night. Bows and crossbows were kept at the stretch, and as we made our way, they kept on a continuous beating of drums and small bells.

The flow of trade was greatly assisted by the advanced money economy which had developed over the centuries. Coins, known as *cash*, were circular pieces of copper, with a hole in the middle, which were tied together with string. The basic unit of currency in the market place was the string of 100 cash, while in the royal treasury the unit was 1,000 cash. In theory the price of articles remained reasonably stable during the period. What happened in fact was that the price of articles did not go up, but the number of coins on the string diminished. So, at the beginning of the Sung period there were about seventy-seven coins in a string of 100 cash, while at the end of the period this had further dropped to about fifty. One of the main problems of China's economy was that there was a serious shortage of copper for the manufacture of these coins. The government tried to counteract this by forbidding the export of coins or copper of any kind, but this order was never obeyed. Attempts were made to issue iron coins, but the metal was altogether too common and so they were never acceptable to the people.

To solve this problem the Chinese hit on the practice of using paper money. As far back as the 9th Century merchants had deposited cash in strong places for safe keeping, and had received receipts in exchange. These receipts then began to change hands in commercial transactions. But this primitive paper money could only be used locally. Then, in the Northern Sung period, the government began to issue notes for transactions in the salt trade. During the Southern Sung period the use of paper money spread rapidly and for the first time the treasury issued notes which were of permanent value and carried the stern warning: 'counterfeiters will be decapitated; the denouncer will be rewarded with 300 strings of cash'.

Some of the emperor's advisers considered that they had found the answer to the nation's financial problems. If the emperor was short of money all he had to do was to print some more. Soon the country was flooded with paper money, and as a result prices began to soar. Confidence in the country's currency began to disappear.

After having for years tried to support and maintain these notes, the people had no longer any confidence in them, and were positively afraid of them. For the payment of government purchases was made in paper. The salaries of all the officials were made in paper. The soldiers received their pay in paper. Of the provinces and districts already in arrear, there was not one that did not discharge its debts in paper. Copper money, which was seldom seen, was considered a treasure. So it was natural that the price of commodities rose, while the value of the paper money fell more and more. This caused the people, already disheartened, to lose all energy.

The Travels of Marco Polo, p. 148.

Few things astonished Marco Polo more than the fact that the Chinese were prepared to accept paper as currency. Coming from the West, he thought it extraordinary that anyone should exchange goods for pieces of paper.

Today the Chinese have a great reputation as traders and businessmen, for, although the mainland is Communist, Chinese tradesmen control much of the wealth of the Far East. This commercial flair is characteristic of the people of the south rather than those of the north. It was natural, therefore, that it should have been fully released during the period of the Southern Sung empire, when the centre of power for the first time lay south of the Yangtze Kiang.

For many centuries Chinese goods had found their way into the markets of the West, but the trade had always been carried on by people of other nationalities. During our era, however, the Chinese began to venture beyond their own shores. They even became a seafaring race. From this trading enterprise a class of wealthy merchants arose. These newly rich men were for a long time shut out of the best society. People of rank did not mix with them, and their sons were, in theory at least, debarred from taking the imperial examinations. Yet they formed an increasingly important element within the community.

The greatest fortunes were put together by those who were successful in overseas trading ventures. For centuries the main trade route between East and West had been the hard and dangerous overland route across central Asia. The fact that all goods had to be carried on the backs of pack animals placed severe restriction on the volume that could be transported. Sea travel was clearly much more economical. During previous centuries there had been flourishing colonies of foreigners – Indians, Arabs, Jews and Persians – in the major ports on the China Sea. The Chinese had looked upon them as barbarians who needed to be civilized. By Sung times these foreign communities were much smaller as Chinese merchants were venturing overseas with their own goods.

The most important exports were textiles and ceramics. In the first category, Chinese silks were sought after by people of fashion across Asia and Europe. Marco Polo was astonished to see cartloads of silk cloth trundling along the roads into the main cities, for sale at a fraction of the price that they would fetch in Venice.

By Sung times potters had raised the art of ceramics to a pitch of perfection barely surpassed before or since. They had learnt how to make dishes which looked 'like ivory, but were as delicate as thin layers of ice'. They made teapots and bowls with delicate fluted edges, incense vases with bold, swirling patterns, delicate boxes patterned with flowers. They worked in subtle shades of cream or ivory as well as bolder purples, crimsons, blues and browns. Large quantities of these beautiful articles were exported every year. The world-wide fame of Chinese ceramics is, of course, best attested by the fact that the word *china* has been adopted in the English language to describe all fine porcelain. During our era, however, the potter himself, within China, was looked upon as a relatively humble craftsman. It was only in later Ming times that, under imperial patronage, ceramics began to receive proper respect as a highly developed art form.

The trading ships returned to Chinese ports laden with goods from other countries; rhinoceros horn, much treasured as a charm and love potion, and ivory from Africa; spices from India and the East Indies; precious stones such as pearl, crystal, agate and coral; rare woods, incense and camphor. Unfortunately for the country's prosperity the balance of trade was unfavourable. That meant that more goods were imported from other countries than were exported out of China. Merchants therefore had to take precious metals, such as gold, silver and copper, with them on their journeys to pay for their purchases. The government tried to stop this drain of wealth, but did not succeed.

Trade was carried in huge seagoing junks, which travelled to Japan, Malaya, India, and as far afield as the east coast of Africa. These vessels, almost square in shape, were propelled by ten pairs of oars, each manned by four oarsmen. The largest carried a crew of 300 men. They had a system of watertight partitions to serve as an added safety factor.

Since the 11th Century Chinese sea captains had had at their disposal that greatest aid to navigation, the magnetic compass. They also understood more conventional methods of setting their ships by the stars as they sailed out of

Examples of Sung ceramics, showing elegance of line and delicate patternwork, which was typical of the period

Porcelain ewer and basin

Stoneware vase   *Stoneware bottle*

sight of land. Chinese sailors had learnt the technique of sailing into the wind, which would not be learnt in Europe for more than a century after the end of the Sung dynasty. The great seagoing junks with sails like 'great clouds in the sky' were therefore technically capable of sailing any of the known oceans. There is, however, no evidence that Chinese captains took their vessels beyond India until the 15th Century. The Chinese had developed the art of map-making further than any other people at the time, but the maps would have been of no great assistance to sea captains, for, while they showed the cities and coastline of China with considerable accuracy, they were extremely vague about the geography of other lands. Although the Chinese had got round to trading with distant countries, they still had little interest in the world outside.

At all levels trade operated under the watchful eye of the state. The power of the emperor was based, not on his military might, but on his control of the country's *water resources*.

> **a** *Rivers and irrigation*. China's basic irrigation structure was maintained by royal officials out of the income from tax. Thus the very productivity of the land depended on the emperor.
>
> **b** *Canals*. He also controlled the canals along which most trading goods were transported from place to place. Therefore, if the emperor had chosen to close the canals, internal trade would almost have come to a standstill.
>
> **c** *The Sea*. Overseas trade was also an imperial monopoly. The emperor controlled the ports and issued permits to particular traders who alone were allowed to deal with the outside world.

All foreign trade had to be conducted through the single port of Canton. When any ship arrived in port the captain had to hand over all his cargo until the last ship of the season's fleet had arrived. Three-tenths of the produce was then held back as customs duty, and the remainder was handed back to the owners. The overseas traders were themselves agents of an imperial monopoly and anyone attempting to trade on his own account was liable to the punishment of branding on the face and exile to an island in the sea.

Those traders who were permitted to travel to other lands brought comparatively few ideas or skills back with them. Since their civilization was more advanced than others that they visited, they felt that they had little to learn. The culture of the Central Nation was complete – a thing in itself. The scholar rulers of China had already formed the policy, which was to infuriate Europeans in the 19th Century, of carrying on trade with other nations while keeping them at arm's length. The 'bamboo curtain' which separates China from the rest of the world, is much older than her present political system.

LINK · The Moguls

To Chinese eyes, then, all foreigners were barbarians. It mattered little whether they belonged to one of the ancient civilizations or whether they were rough nomads from the northern grasslands. In the same way that they were prepared to trade with Arabians, Persians or Indians, so they were prepared to do business with the true barbarians beyond the Great Wall. A brisk trade passed north and south, and, unlike the seagoing trade with the rest of the world, its balance was strongly tilted in favour of the Chinese.

The nomads, inhabiting a land with an annual rainfall of less than twenty inches, looked to their herds to provide them with food, clothing and shelter. These were the barest necessities of life. But they soon discovered that the people in the civilized land to the south possessed manufactured goods – and particularly those made of iron – which could make living a great deal easier. In return they could provide horses, which were never successfully reared in China. This trade would have worked to the benefit of both sides, except that the nomads had more need for manufactured goods than the Chinese had for horses. They were always tempted to invade the civilized lands across the Great Wall and take away the goods that they wanted without paying for them.

There was a second serious problem about life on the grasslands. Since the soil was poor, the land would only support a limited number of people. But human population has a natural tendency to expand. If the number of people exceeds the capacity of the land to support them, there is bound to be starvation. Over the centuries the nomads had developed an effective, if drastic, method of keeping their own numbers in check. The tribes lived in a continuous state of warfare among themselves, and it was recognized practice that, when one tribe defeated its enemy, it would kill off all the males and enslave the women and children.

Two occurrences could upset the balance. In the first place an adverse climatic change might make the steppes even more dry and infertile than usual. Then the people had the alternative of killing each other off at an even faster rate than was customary, or breaking out of their homeland and invading the more fertile countries around their border. It is difficult to trace climatic changes in the past with any certainty, but it is possible that such a change has taken place twice in recorded history. The first of these helped to bring about the end of the Roman Empire; the second occurred in the 13th Century AD. The other way in which the balance could be upset was if a strong leader emerged to unify the nomad peoples so that they stopped fighting among

Jenghiz Khan

themselves. Such a leader had to make war against other countries, both to counteract the increase in population which was bound to take place when the tribes stopped fighting one another and to provide an outlet for the warlike habits which his people had developed over so many centuries. Chinese emperors were well aware of this danger. From one dynasty to the next, they had therefore followed a consistent policy of using every possible device to ensure that the tribes remained divided among themselves.

In the last years of the 12th Century the greatest leader that the nomads ever had began to bring the tribes under a single authority. Temujan was the son of a minor chieftain – legend had it that he was born with a ball of clotted

68

blood in his fist, which was read as a sign that he would grow up to be a great warrior. As a young man he soon proved himself an outstanding general. His tribe overcame its enemies and before long other tribes began to come of their own accord to fight under Temujan's banner of the nine yaks' tails. By the year 1206 thirty-one tribes had united under his leadership and his power was unchallenged across a thousand miles of grassland. In that year he assumed the title of Jenghiz Khan, by which he was to become known and feared throughout Asia. Jenghiz Khan fought, not for plunder, but for the glory of victory. His early successes had led him to believe that he was rightfully the ruler of the whole world. Anyone who stood against him had therefore to be destroyed without mercy. He is reported to have summed up his ambition in the words:

> Man's highest joy is in victory: to conquer one's enemies, to pursue them, to deprive them of their possessions, to make their beloved weep, to ride on their horses and to embrace their wives and daughters.

Although his dominions were wide, the total number of his followers could not have been far above a million – or about the population of Hanchow. From these he could muster some quarter of a million fighting men.

The Moguls had short bow legs and longish bodies. Their faces were distinctive, with their high cheekbones, flat noses and eyes narrowed by the sun and wind. They lived in beehive tents made of felt, eating meat, milk and blood provided by the animals that they tended. Marco Polo, who had ample opportunity of seeing their way of life at first hand, left this description.

> They have circular houses made of wood and covered with felt, which they carry about with them on four-wheeled wagons wherever they go. For the framework of rods is so neatly and skilfully constructed that it is light to carry. And every time they unfold their house and set it up, the door is always facing south. They also have excellent two-wheeled carts covered with black felt, of such good design that if it rained all the time the rain would never wet anything in the cart. These are drawn by oxen and camels. And in these carts they carry their wives and children and all they need in the way of utensils.
>
> *The Travels of Marco Polo*, pp. 97–8.

Although comparatively few in number, the Moguls had certain great assets as warriors. In the first place their armies were completely mobile. Since they could live off their animals, they had no problems of supply. Again, Marco Polo described how they set off on an expedition.

> When they are going on a long expedition, they carry no baggage with them. They each carry two leather flasks to hold the milk they drink and a small pot for cooking meat. They also carry a small tent to shelter them from the rain. In case of need, they will ride a good ten days' journey without provisions and without making a fire, living only on the blood of their horses; for every rider pierces a vein of his horse and drinks the blood. They also have their dried milk, which is solid like paste; and this is how they dry it. First they bring the milk to the boil. At the appropriate moment they skim off the cream that floats on the surface and put it in another vessel to be made into butter, because so long as it remained the milk could not be dried. Then they stand the milk in the sun and leave it to dry. When they are going on an expedition, they take about ten pounds of this milk; and every morning they take out about half a pound of it and put it in a small leather flask, shaped like a gourd, with as much water as they please. Then, while they ride, the milk in the flask dissolves into a fluid, which they drink. And this is their breakfast.
>
> *The Travels of Marco Polo*, pp. 100–1.

They could therefore cover great distances and appear when least expected.

They were also accustomed to living by a ferocious code of law, which demanded absolute obedience on pain of death. The Khan could therefore expect a far higher degree of loyalty from his followers than could a Chinese general from his unwilling soldiers. When we consider the dreadful cruelties which the Moguls inflicted on others, it is important to remember that they were only doing to others what they had long done to one another.

Jenghiz Khan's warriors wore sheepskin jackets and armour of lacquered leather. Those who could afford it also wore shirts of raw silk. When an arrow went into his body the silk of the shirt did not tear and the wounded man was therefore able to pull the arrow out without inflicting too much damage on himself. They carried a hooked lance, a curved sword, and two bows, one for use on horseback and one for use on foot. They also had arrows of three different sizes and weights for use according to the distance and armour of the enemy. The rest of their equipment consisted of an axe, needles and thread, a rope, a kit for sharpening arrows, spare clothes carried in a watertight skin, a cooking pot, and some dried meat and curds.

The tribes under Jenghiz Khan's rule were allocated different areas of pasture land. Each chief was responsible for keeping his men in constant readiness for war. Fighting units were organized on the decimal basis. The smallest unit was the *file* of ten men; the largest, the *touman* of 10,000. Between these there were intermediate commands of 100 and 1,000. When advancing into enemy territory, Mogul troops moved on a broad front, but the greatest care was taken to ensure that they remained in touch with each other. The Khan's special messengers, or 'arrow riders', were trained to cover immense distances. They bandaged their bodies to give them support, and it was said that they were able to sleep in the saddle. These arrow riders were given the best horses in the army and, in a crisis, their needs were met before those of anyone else.

'March divided – fight united': this motto was the key to much of the success of the Mogul armies. Generally they found themselves confronted by much larger forces. By keeping his army split up until the last minute, Jenghiz Khan was able to keep opposing generals uncertain about where the main attack would fall. When he did strike, his whole force was pitted against a single objective. Often the first devastating blow was enough to destroy the enemy. If this failed, his men fell back on well-planned manoeuvres.

> When they join battle with their enemies, these are the tactics by which they prevail. They are never ashamed to have recourse to flight. They manoeuvre freely, shooting at the enemy, now from this quarter, now from that. They have trained their horses so well that they wheel this way or that as quickly as a dog would do. When they are pursued and take to flight, they fight as well and as effectively as when they are face to face

Mogul cavalry pursue a fleeing army

with the enemy. When they are fleeing at top speed, they twist round with their bows and let fly their arrows to such good purpose that they kill the horses of the enemy and the riders too. When the enemy thinks he has routed and crushed them, then he is lost; for he finds his horses killed and not a few of his men. As soon as the Tartars decide that they have killed enough of the pursuing horses and horsemen, they wheel round and attack and acquit themselves so well and so courageously that they gain a complete victory. By these tactics they have already won many battles and conquered many nations.

The Travels of Marco Polo, p. 101.

In 1207, a year after assuming his title, Jenghiz Khan led his followers against the semi-barbarian kingdom of Hsi-Hsia. His men were completely successful in the field, but, for the first time, he came up against the problem of how to capture walled cities. During the next years the Moguls began to learn the arts of siege warfare. In 1211 the hordes crossed the Great Wall in a full-scale attack on the Chin Empire of Northern China. The Chin people had lost their military instincts in the century since they destroyed Hui Tsung's empire. In four years of campaigning Jenghiz was therefore able to devastate Northern China. In 1216 he consented to be bought off, and returned to the Mogul homeland, laden with booty. Among his trophies were many Chinese craftsmen, who would teach their skills to his people, and also scholars, who were set to work to reduce the Mogul language to written form.

Fortunately for the people of Southern China, Jenghiz Khan next turned his attention towards the West. In an outstandingly successful campaign he swept across Central Asia. In 1220 he captured the ancient caravan city of Samarkand. He then moved onwards, until he came up against the Moslem empires of the Middle East. Still he was successful, and by 1224 he had destroyed the ancient civilization of Persia. He then returned east to campaign uncomfortably close to the Chinese frontier. In the autumn of 1227, while besieging the capital city of West Hsia, the great conqueror received the wounds from which he died. His followers completed the capture of the city, massacred every human being inside it, and then withdrew to their homeland to begin the long process of choosing a successor. Their choice fell on Ughetai, who proved no less formidable a warrior than Jenghiz. In the twelve years of his reign he carried Mogul power across Russia and into Eastern Europe. It is interesting to speculate how different the future history of the world would have been had the hordes continued their drive towards the Atlantic. The issue between the light horsemen from the steppes and the cumbersome knights of medieval Europe was never put to the test. Compared to the rich empires of China, India and the Middle East, Europe was a backward area, hardly worth invading.

By the time of Ughetai's death the Mogul Empire had spread out to cover such a wide area that it could no longer be ruled by one man. It therefore divided into four. For half a century China had been left in peace, while the Moguls conquered in the West. With the division of the Empire each ruler had the desire to increase his own lands. In 1260, therefore, Kublai Khan, Great Khan of the Far East, decided to make good his claim to be ruler of the whole of China.

Kublai Khan

The fifty years of respite proved to be most important for the future of Chinese civilization, for the horsemen who now rode across the rice fields of the China plain were not the mindless destroyers that had followed Jenghiz. While overrunning semi-civilized empires like Hsi-Hsia and West Hsia, the Moguls had themselves begun to learn Chinese ways. They now had, therefore, a certain respect for the country they conquered. Nevertheless their coming struck fear into the peaceful Chinese. In a display of courage one official put up a poster in Nanking, declaring, 'If the horsemen of the north arrive, I am prepared to die rather than flee'. But by the time that the Moguls arrived he had taken himself to safety and was nowhere to be seen. The invaders therefore changed his words to read, 'If I cannot conquer them, I shall flee'.

73

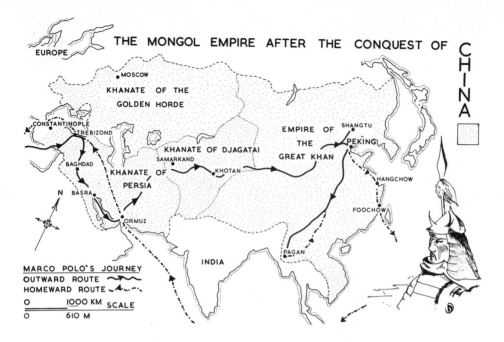

THE MONGOL EMPIRE AFTER THE CONQUEST OF CHINA

EUROPE

MOSCOW

KHANATE OF THE
GOLDEN HORDE

CONSTANTINOPLE
TREBIZOND

KHANATE OF DJAGATAI

EMPIRE OF
THE
GREAT KHAN

SHANGTU

PEKING

BAGHDAD
SAMARKAND
KHOTAN

KHANATE OF
PERSIA

HANGCHOW

N   BASRA

FOOCHOW

ORMUZ

PAGAN

INDIA

MARCO POLO'S JOURNEY
OUTWARD ROUTE
HOMEWARD ROUTE
0   1000 KM SCALE
0   610 M

For some years the soft civilization of the Southern Sung was cushioned by the Chin kingdom in the north. But this time the invaders were not be halted on the Yangtze River. Hanchow fell to Kublai's army in 1275. From that time onwards something of the sparkle was lacking from the life of that great city. The new Mogul – who founded the dynasty known as *Yuan* – insisted on greater discipline of life. While before the sounds of entertainment had gone on long into the night, men now had to be indoors by curfew. But when Marco Polo visited Hanchow a few years later, he found that the crowds teemed in the Imperial Way, and the carts brought goods into market, as in the days of the Sung emperors. And the Mogul conquerors, for their part, were becoming more Chinese every day. The old story had been repeated. It was a comparatively easy task for invaders to defeat the vast, disorganized body which passed for the Chinese army. But China again demonstrated its vast reserves of strength, which were rooted in the teachings of Confucian philosophers and in the family traditions of common folk. Civilization finally triumphed over barbarism and the scholars and ancestors of China proved more than a match for the brute strength of the Mogul hordes.

Index